TO PA
MAy your Life be
STress free!

FIRST
RESPONDERS
HANDBOOK
OF HUMOR

Best wishes

HICKS—JORDAN

Quiet Man Publishing ™

Quiet Man Publishing TM

ISBN 13: 978-0-9742829-3-0
ISBN 10: 0-9742829-3-6

Library of Congress copyright registration on file.

Cover art by Miguel Romo
Jacket design by Budget Book Design
M.A.S.H © Fox Television
Copyright © 2005 John B. Hicks and Dan Jordan
Published 2006
For more information, please visit us on the web at
www.quietmanpublishing.com

First Edition

10 9 8 7 6 5 4 3 2 1

COVERING OUR REAR DISCLAIMER

The following stories are based on actual events. Only some names have been changed to protect the innocent and the just plain guilty. This book is intended to offer first responders affected with overwhelming stress a chance to recognize that their reactions are normal and also to offer some practical advice on how to cope with stress. It is not meant to take the place of regular psychological counseling. All views and opinions expressed and all advice given in this book are the views, opinions, and advice of the authors, and not necessarily of their respected departments or sponsors...blah, blah, blah.

The appropriateness of any view, opinion, or advice offered in this book will depend on your individual situation. We recommend that you consult with professional advisors; such as tax, legal, medical, financial, mechanical, psychological, spiritual, taxidermy, or veterinary before implementing any opinions or advice given in this book. DUH!

Possible side effects of reading this book:

- Laughing until you leak!
- Having a better outlook on your life and career.
- Indigestion!

No animals were hurt during the writing of this book.

FOREWORD

by Marlee Matlin, Award-Winning Actress

Photo © Jeff Katz

"I have always resisted putting limitations on myself,
both professionally and personally."

—Marlee Matlin

When one thinks of the life of a first responder, the first thing that comes to mind could be a scene taken from a Hollywood movie—a firefighter rushing into a burning building to save a child's life, a police officer arriving just in time to stop a robbery, a paramedic starting life-saving techniques to revive a dying patient. You may think these are all just parts from a movie, but the truth is they really *do* happen and at a very high price to the men and women we call "first responders." As the wife of a police officer, I have witnessed first hand the reality of their world: the long hours they work, the lost time away from their family, the physical demands of the job which could result in injury, and even the possibility none of us likes to think about—the ultimate sacrifice of losing one's life in the line of duty.

There is one other hazard, though, that most people, even first responders, are not even aware of—stress. Stress not only affects the first responders themselves, but also the ones they love. The *First Responders Handbook of Humor* provides simple techniques to help first responders and their families deal with the stress and helps lift the spirit in a most unlikely fashion – through humor. The *First Responders Handbook of Humor* offers amusing and heartwarming tales from first responders from around the world as a means to show everyone that laughter is often the best medicine. As a mother, actress, author, and wife of a first responder, I know we are all constantly looking for ways to balance out the stress in our lives; The *First Responders Handbook of Humor* allows the necessary insight to accomplish this.

— Marlee Matlin, Wife of a First Responder

MINI-BIOGRAPHY

Marlee Matlin received worldwide critical acclaim for her motion picture debut in Paramount Pictures' "Children of a Lesser God." In 1994, Marlee was appointed by President Clinton and confirmed by the Senate to the Board of Directors for the Corporation for National Service. In 1995, Marlee served as Chairperson for National Volunteer Week and honored in a White House Rose Garden ceremony by the President. Marlee currently serves as a national celebrity spokesperson for The American Red Cross, encouraging Americans to donate blood in light of recent tragedies like Hurricane Katrina. She has also worked on behalf of closed captioning and in 1990 was instrumental in getting Congress to pass federal legislation requiring all televisions manufactured in the United States be equipped with closed captioning technology so familiar to us today. She also serves on the boards of a number of charitable organizations including VSA Arts, Easter Seals, The Children Affected by Aids Foundation, The Elizabeth Glaser Pediatric Aids Foundation, Best Buddies, as well as those charities which primarily benefit children. Marlee has also combined her charity work with commercial ventures and has appeared in numerous commercials and Public Service Announcements each designed to raise awareness about the importance of donating to charitable organizations.

www.marleematlinsite.com

TRUE CONFESSIONS

A heartfelt thank you to my beautiful wife, Lisa, and our two children, Justin and Alison, for allowing me the time to pursue my dream of writing this book. To Tracy Healy, thanks for pointing out our mistakes. To K. Martin, J. Carmichael, J. Martinez and J. Segovia, thanks for listening to me complain and brag about the progress of the book. To my brother and sister first responders who have my back.
    —Dan Jordan

To my wife, Nancy. Thank you for all the help in getting it right. I will love you forever and always, and all the time in between! To Miguel Romo. Thanks for the great cover art. Keep the dream alive!
    —John Hicks

In Loving Memory

Hagop "Jake" Kuredjian, 60M2

Los Angeles County Sheriff's Department
Date of Birth: June 5, 1961
Appointed: February 1, 1984

Award: Gold Meritorious Conduct Medal in 1989 for rescuing a
woman from a cliff in Malibu, CA.

Tour of Duty: 17 years
End of Watch: August 31, 2001, age 40

Hero: *A person noted for feats of courage or nobility of purpose,
especially one who has risked or sacrificed his or her life.*

Deputy Jake Kuredjian is a special hero that has touched many lives. Through his living and passing, he has taught us the value of life. Take these memories and become a more warm, loving, and caring person. By reinvesting in life and sharing love with others, you will honor this hero who made the ultimate sacrifice. In so doing, he will never be forgotten.

BEHIND EVERY MAN IS A STORY. BEHIND EVERY STORY ARE TEARS!

August 31, 2001: A team of approximately twelve officers from the Bureau of Alcohol, Tobacco, and Firearms and the U.S. Marshals, along with deputies from the Los Angeles County Sheriff's Department arrived at the residence of a warrant suspect who was a twice-convicted felon. The suspect was wanted for impersonating an officer and for possession of illegal firearms. The suspect refused to come out of the house and opened fire on the officers with an automatic weapon. Deputy Kuredjian, a motorcycle officer (60M2) and 17 year veteran of the Los Angles County Sheriff's Department, responded to the assistance call of shots fired. Upon arrival, Deputy Kuredjian stopped four doors east of the suspect's location and ducked for cover behind a nearby car. Deputy Kuredjian was fatally shot by the suspect from the second floor of his home using a high powered scoped rifle. The suspect then held other officers at bay for several hours. The suspect died after tear gas canisters ignited the house causing it to become a fiery tomb, burning the home to the ground.

"Courage is not the absence of fear, but rather the judgment that something else is more important than fear."

—Ambrose Redmoon (1933-1996) Writer

9

ANATOMY OF ACRONYMS

(Why is "abbreviation" such a long word?)

ALS	Advance Life Support
Ambu bag	Disposable Bag Used for Artificial Respirations
AMR	American Medical Response
BLS	Basic Life Support
CPR	Cardiopulmonary Resuscitation
Capt.	Captain
Det.	Detective
D.O.A	Dead on Arrival
EMS	Emergency Medical Service
EMT-B	Emergency Medical Technician-Basic
EMT-P	Emergency Medical Technician-Paramedic
ENG	Engineer
FF	Firefighter
FF/PM	Firefighter/Paramedic
FD	Fire Department
IV	Intravenous Line
IV	Roman Numeral Four
Lt.	Lieutenant
OEC	Outdoor Emergency Care
PD	Police Department
POW	Prisoner of War
RN	Registered Nurse
Ret.	Retired
Trd.	Tired
TWP	Township
K-9	Canine
V.I.N.	Vehicle Identification Number

OPERATING TABLE OF CONTENTS

INTRODUCTION

Q: Who must do the difficult things?
A: Those who can.
— Japanese Riddle

Police officers, firefighters and emergency medical technicians—America's first responders—are, and always will be in a tough and stressful occupation. In addition to the ever-increasing dangers of today's world, along with the related stress from post 9/11 terrorism, there now appears to be even more severe sources of stress for our first responders than ever before. With the increased attention and criticism from the media, public anxiety and loss of morale because of layoffs, reduced benefits and no pay raises due to government and departmental budget crisis, these everyday challenges are quickly building on the shoulders of today's heroes. Even positive change for first responder's depart-ments, such as new and increased anti-terrorism training, has increased the stress for personnel by adding to already rigorous assignments. It is also becoming increasingly clear that the business of first responding exacts a severe toll on the responder's own family, bringing with it serious consequences. Stress among first responder personnel and their families can add to an already stressful home environment, impairing one's ability to perform his or her job in a safe and effective manner.

"I happen to believe there can be no definition of a successful life
that does not include service to others."
—George Bush, 41st President of the United States

12

In response to this, we have created this book to address these very issues. This book is based in part on a workshop developed by Dan Jordan called, "The Magic to Balancing Stress." Dan has taken to speaking nationally, presenting strategies to first responders to help balance job stress and the impact it has on their families. In addition to the basic stress reduction tips and ideas presented, he also introduces a formula to balancing stress called the "Triad of Balance." This formula, consisting of creativity, humor, and playfulness, can effectively balance one's stress in life and work. Sure, an emergency operation is no laughing matter, but, when the "Triad" is properly applied, these tools can, and already have, successfully helped first responders deal positively with the stress from unusual occurrences at work, job related problems, and other similar situations. Whereas, it is advisable and sometimes very easy for civilians and their families to avoid some types of stress, it isn't always as simple for first responders. The "Triad of Balance," however, can be an effective survival tool in dealing with the unforeseen stress that can't be avoided. This book was developed with a desire to help other first responders rediscover the happy side to their jobs and life! Thank you to all who have contributed stories to this book and, in the process, started on the journey to a balanced life. We trust you will enjoy the incredible, true and humorous stories from the men and women that we call first responders, working daily to protect the public on our nation's front lines!

BUL – YAW! (Balance Ur Life – You'll Always Win!")
—Dan Jordan, Deputy Sheriff - John Hicks, Firefighter/Paramedic

STRESS 101

So, what is this thing called, "STRESS?" Well, stress is the body's response to any demand or pressure, especially when demands exceed one's resources. Any change requiring adaptation, even positive change creates stress. For first responders, any situation that causes them to experience strong emotional reactions, either at the scene of an emergency, or later on, will create a stressful response.

Stress is a natural and highly adaptive biological process that strengthens and safeguards us in many ways. It has been part of our chemical make up for thousands of years, helping prehistoric humans survive by enabling them to run faster or fight harder; often called the "fight or flight" response. The net effect of stress on the body is the release of cortisol and other hormones that essentially breaks down the body's cells in an effort to provide it with an emergency supply of energy and strength, temporarily sharpening mental skills, heightening concentration and jolting the body into a state of alertess. As a result, a person under stress may perform better.

In an emergency, these hormones come in handy, but over time, these same hormones can cause an imbalance in personal long-term health. Today, our struggle for survival more often involves chronic (ongoing) sources of stress, such as personnel conflicts in the work place, traffic jams, hectic schedules, and credit card debt. Chronic stress creates "wear and tear" on the body, breaking it down and making the person sick in many ways. Stress requires the person to make adjustments physically, psychologically, socially and even spiritually, to maintain the necessary balance for survival.

"If your stress mounts so high that you begin snapping at people, ask yourself, "Is it worth having a Heart Attack over this?"
—Dr. Murray Mittleman

A common side-effect of stress at work is "burnout." Some psychologists refer to burnout as "compassion fatigue," a deep physical, emotional and spiritual exhaustion accompanied by acute emotional pain. However, no matter what you call it, one of stress / burnout's most perilous aspects is that, while it's easy to recognize it in someone else, you may miss seeing it in your own life! This is because stress / burnout often creeps into your life. Those who have been affected often describe the stress / burnout syndrome as a feeling of being sucked into a vortex that pulls them slowly downward, and they have no idea how to stop it. First responders in this perilous position often cope by working even harder and continuing to give to others until they're completely tapped out!

Studies have shown that one in four workers suffers from an anxiety related illness.(*Think of three friends at work. If they're okay, then you're it!) If left unchanged, job related stress may soon be the number one reason cited for workers' compensation claims. If you are sensing stress / burnout in your life, sound the alarm and douse the fire.

FAST FACT

U.S. workers consume 15 tons of aspirin a day!
(Not per person)

Remember as a child a parent telling you never to talk to strangers? Well, that Golden Rule doesn't apply to first responders; they are required to talk to strangers on a daily basis in the performance of their duties. Not only do they have to talk to strangers, but they also have to assist them in time of need, arrest them, treat their injuries (real and fake), and rescue them from their own stupidity. Let's face it, the business of first responders—law enforcement, firefighting, and emergency medical treatment—is very stressful! When stressors are prolonged and overwhelming, an individual's ability to cope becomes difficult. Too much stress, too often, can reduce one's performance and be unhealthy. Causes of extreme stress can include, but is not limited to, physically dangerous jobs, rotating shift work, long hours, exposure to violence and human suffering, poor supervision, lack of career opportunities, inadequate rewards, excessive paperwork, poor equipment, fear and danger. The result of this overwhelming stress is alarming, often leading to depression, alcoholism, domestic violence, high divorce rates, heart attacks, cancer, and suicide. First responders are not bulletproof to stress. With frequent and close encounters to human depravity and human suffering, the first responders' continued exposure to extreme stress can have a number of damaging physical and emotional effects.

STRESS MYTH #1
No Symptoms = No Stress

The absence of symptoms does not mean the absence of stress. In fact, camouflaging symptoms with medication such as aspirin, may deprive you of the warning signals needed for reducing the strain of your stress.

Generally, stress will affect a person three ways: Emotionally, Socially and Physically. Common symptoms of these are:

Emotional Effects of Stress:
1) Depression, anxiety, nervousness, tension, irritability
2) Moodiness, negative attitude, hopelessness, guilt
3) Lethargy, lack of motivation and creativity
4) Confusion, forgetfulness, inability to concentrate

Social Effects of Stress:
1) Loneliness, isolating oneself from others
2) Emotional detachment, lack of communication
3) Cynicism, suspiciousness, hostility, lashing out
4) Increase in the use of alcohol, suicide
5) Low productivity, increase in sick days

Physical Effects of Stress:
1) Nausea, vomiting, diarrhea, ulcers
2) Colds, influenza, skin irritation and cold sores
3) Quickening heart rate, increased blood pressure
4) Changes in eating patterns/sleeping patterns, insomnia
5) Difficultly breathing, heart attacks
6) Headaches, muscle aches, clenching of the jaw,
   grinding of the teeth, decreased libido

"Of the adults who go to doctor's offices, 5-9% complaining of common problems like back pain or headaches are also suffering from a serious underlying condition: STRESS"

STRESS MYTH #2
Only major symptoms of stress require attention.
Minor symptoms, such as headaches, or stomach aches can be early warnings that your life if getting out of hand and that you need to do a better job of managing the stress.

SELF-ASSESSMENT TEST FOR STRESS:

How stressed are you?
Find out your stress level by taking this stress quiz.

*This self-test has not been validated and is not intended to provide medical advice or diagnosis. The results should only serve as a quick check of your state of mind and condition of life. Consult a physician or mental health professional if you think you might be suffering from stress.

Carefully consider each of the following statements by answering yes or no:

1. Personal concerns commonly intrude on my professional role.

2. My colleagues seem to lack understanding.

3. I feel little compassion towards most of my co-workers.

4. I feel estranged from others.

5. I have recently thought that I need more close friends.

6. I have often thought that I am not succeeding at achieving my life's goals.

7. I find it difficult to separate my personal life from my work life.

8. I find even small changes extremely difficult.

9. I can't seem to recover quickly after association with trauma.

10. There is normally no one to talk with about highly stressful experiences.

11. I have recently thought that I need to "work through" a traumatic experience in my life.

12. I force myself to avoid certain thoughts or feelings that remind me of a frightening experience.

13. I feel a sense of hopefulness.

14. I have a sense of disillusionment associated with my work.

15. I have outbursts of anger or irritability with little provocation.

16. I feel weak, tired, and rundown as a result of my work as a first responder.

17. I currently feel depressed as a result of my work as a first responder.

18. I often have trouble focusing my thoughts, remembering things, or making decisions.

19. I don't sleep well.

20. I can't remember what I use to do for fun.

Answering "yes" to six or more of these questions may indicate that you are suffering from overwhelming stress.

Question:

What do you call a person that says they don't have any stress in their life?

Answer:

Dead or in Denial! (Not the river in Egypt)

(In Los Angeles there is a hot line for people in denial…so far no one has called!) If you are in denial about your stress, then buy our next book titled, *"Better Living Through Denial."* Or just continue to read on with an open mind since you already paid $14.00 for this one!

In addition to on the job stressors that a first responder faces, he or she must also deal with the common, everyday stressors faced by most individuals during their lifetime (i.e., one's aging and poor health, illness or injury of a loved one, money concerns and relationship problems).

The combination of job and personal stress not only affects the first responder, but can also take a tremendous toll on the people closest to them, including family members. In one study of 479 spouses of police officers, 77% reported experiencing unusually high amounts of stress from the officer's job. Commonly stated reasons included:

- Disruption of family activities due to shift work
- Fear that the officer will be hurt or killed
- The officer's perceived paranoia
- Overprotection of family members

"It probably won't be a bullet that strikes down a police officer, but the cumulative effects of job stress."
—Unknown

One way or another, it seems that first responders almost always find a way to deal with the stress in their lives. Unfortunately, a lot of first responders find unhealthy ways to cope with the stress, including abuse of drugs, alcohol, food, sex, and work. Most people recognize the negative effects of drugs, alcohol, and food. Now, before you giggle at the thought of "abuse of sex," consider its meaning and ramifications. Sometimes people are so overwhelmed by the stress in their lives; they become depressed, and start looking for a little slice of happiness by cheating on their spouse. This small glimmer of happiness from their wrongful tryst, however, can eventually lead to more and greater stress. Keep in mind that *marriage is grand; divorce a hundred grand!*

Let's talk about work now. Though most of us dislike the thought of working too much, that is exactly what many of us do when we are stressed. It is not uncommon for one to work as much as possible in order to escape problems at home. At work, we tend to have more control over things, even though a majority of personal stress comes from one's occupation. Another reason people try to escape the stress through work is that work is a constant, and something the person is familiar with. Work tends to be a comfort zone for many people even though most are uncomfortable in their comfort zone.

Even more disturbing than the coping methods previously described, is the unhealthy way of terminating the stress through suicide. In an FBI report, it stated that more police officers commit suicide than are killed by criminals! According to the Census Bureau in San Francisco, from 1987 to 1997, the general population's suicide rate was 21 per 100,000. For police officers in the same ten year period, the rate was 33.3 per 100,000. Groups that track police suicides estimate that a police officer kills himself or herself every 24 to 52 hours. Shortly after September 11, 2001, at least nine first responders involved in rescue and recovery efforts have committed suicide. According to an analysis by the Occupational Safety & Health Administration (OSHA), at least 100 police officers and paramedics committed suicide while on the job between 1992-2001.

The exact number of suicides among rescue workers may never fully be known. This is in part because suicide in general is underreported and because OSHA tracks only on-the-job deaths. Moreover, many states do not track deaths by occupation, making it nearly impossible to determine and/or study suicide rates of first responders.

The cumulative negative effects of stress on the first responders and their families have also effected their departments in negative ways such as:

- Tardiness and absenteeism
- Reduced individual efficiency in performing duties
- Reduced departmental productivity
- Stress related early retirements or long term disability

TOP 5 CAUSES OF EARLY RETIREMENT:

- Job related stress
- Repressed emotions
- High exposure to human misery
- Too many sacrifices (both emotionally and physically)
- Inadequate departmental support

Among people whose job it is to save others, it is especially hard for them to ask for help, even though it is readily available to them. Because they are often the first to recognize when a first responder needs help, family members can play a crucial role in encouraging the first responder to seek assistance before the problem becomes severe. A number of departments and agencies have responded positively and productively to the problem of first responder stress by providing short and long term counseling, critical incident stress debriefing, crisis intervention, and by establishing stress reduction training and peer support. Some of these programs are also offered to family members of first responders.

"We don't reach out for help, we are the helpers!"
-Anonymous

All these stress management programs are a step in the right direction in giving support and help to first responders, but is it enough? An argument could be made for more training on preventing stress and stress related problems. The training needs to focus on the first responder's ability to recognize sources and signs of stress and to develop strategies for coping. Many experts believe that the basic training academy is the best time to begin such teachings. This then should be followed up by providing regular in-service training to reinforce these concepts and strategies. However, the focus at the basic training academy is on the tools of the trade, department policies, rules, and laws governing such agencies and personnel. Very few training academies offer any training or resources to help their personnel cope with the job related stresses they will encounter in their forthcoming public service careers. In the following pages, we will provide you with practical ideas and tips to mitigate stress in order to "stress less." This book will introduce you to the "Triad of Balance," a necessary tool to balance the stress in one's life and career.

"You cannot live a perfect day without doing something for someone, who will never be able to repay you."
John Wooden - College Basketball Coach

Could This Be Stress?

QUESTION:
Is stress the same for everyone?

. . .A very good question. Read the following story and we will then give you the answer.

TAXES, a stressful subject for sure! Pretty much everyone hates taxes (love Texas!) except the government. Taxes fall into two main categories, income tax and property tax. As a child, First Responder Hans Zupp remembers the month of April very well. That was when his dad would lock himself in the family room to compile and compute the family income taxes. Hearing his dad complaining through the closed door, Zupp was able to add some new four-letter words to his vocabulary. Skip ahead many years later. Zupp came home from work to find a letter from a government agency known nationally by its three initials, IRS. The letter read in brief, "Dear Mr. Zupp, you are being audited. Thank you and have a nice day!" It turned out to be a general audit and the IRS wanted to see three consecutive years of back taxes, receipts, canceled checks, and proof of deductions. Based on a suggestion, Zupp allowed his accountant to represent him at the audit. This was so his personal stressful attitude wouldn't interfere and cause more problems. So Zupp provided all the tax documents he had stored away, including a few deductible receipts compliments of friends at work, to his accountant who went to battle on his behalf. With all the necessary documents now in the accountant's hands, Zupp then began the very long, stressful wait to see how much he would owe. Doubts started drifting in and out of his consciousness. Did he give the accountant the right documents? Did he forget an important receipt? Many stressful weeks passed before he received another letter from the IRS explaining that the audit was now complete and that he owed them a whopping $6,600! That's right, six-thousand-six- hundred dollars! His stress level started rising up to his receding hair line! "Not to worry," his accountant said. "We can appeal." His accountant then marched back into the auditor's office, again without Zupp's help or hindrance, to argue his tax deductions and audit results. Many stressful weeks went by before he heard any news back about there count. Finally, the second IRS notification came in the mail. Zupp quickly opened the letter to find that his tax bill had been reduced to $3,700. Now sure, this is a substantial reduction of the initial audit, however, it was still a bill he really didn't want to pay. With his stress level way up, he decided to pay the bill to be done with this "losing contest of patriotism."

One person's stressor is another's challenge
—Dan Jordan by personal experience

Based on the same stressful situation, if Bill Gates, the founder and president of Microsoft, (oxymoron—Microsoft Works) and one of the richest men in the world, was audited and had to pay $3,700, he probably wouldn't have the same stress about it as Hans Zupp did. In fact, he would most likely have his people pay it for him or pay it out of his front pocket.

So, to answer the question, "Is stress the same for everyone?" the answer is, NO! What is stressful for one person may not be stressful for another. Stress level for first responders will likely differ based on the individual's experiences, time on the job, type of training received, financial stability, and the access to a strong social network and coping resources. The stress level will also vary based on two main components of stress: Attitude and Perception. Your stress is about your "ATTITUDE" and your "PERCEPTION".

"50% of the Solution is Defining the Problem" – Dr. Phil

ATTITUDE 101

"You can't direct the wind, but you can adjust your sails"
—Author unknown

Attitude is based on your beliefs, feelings, and point of view. Attitude is shown in tone of voice, facial expressions, handwriting, posture, your handshake, and even your voice-mail message. In every situation, your attitude seeps through. Stress is in part, the attitude or mindset you bring to things. We are in charge of our own attitudes, and everyday we can make a choice regarding it. There are always two attitudes you can choose to bring to a situation: a positive attitude or a negative attitude. There is a saying by author and Pastor Charles Swindoll, that "Life is 10% of what happens to you and 90% how you react to it!" So, it's not what happens to you that determines your happiness, but rather the attitude you choose on how to deal with it.

"Success in life is based more on mental attitude than capability!"
—Author unknown

The famous author of the book, "The Power of Positive Thinking," Norman Vincent Peale, once said, "There is a basic law that like attracts like, negative thinking attracts negative results. Conversely, if a person routinely thinks optimistically and hopefully, his positive thinking sets in motion creative forces and success. Instead of eluding him, it will flow towards him."

"A man is but a product of his thoughts; what he thinks he becomes"
—Mohandas K. Gandi

The problem that gets in the way of choosing a positive attitude is that we have developed a habit of worrying too much. Worry comes from our imagination run amuck!

The following joke told to a dad by his seven-year-old daughter illustrates this point. "Daddy," the girl asked, "Imagine you are in a jungle being chased by a giraffe, surrounded by tigers, laughed at by a pack of hyenas, and stalked by a lion. What do you do?" "I don't know?" the dad replied. The daughter answered, "Stop Imagining!"

Basically, the game of "what if" has gotten way out of control in our thinking. WHAT IF I have to work on the weekend? WHAT IF I have to work with someone I dislike? WHAT IF I get a citizen complaint today?

"I have never seen a monument erected to a pessimist"
- Paul Harvey - Radio Commentator

Having a positive attitude is something you should strive for. It isn't something you are or are not, it is something you can become. The happiest people don't necessarily have the best of everything; they just make the best of everything. It all comes down to attitude. We all hold attitudes about many subjects important to us personally, and we cannot simply decide to change those feelings and attitudes and it's done. We can, however, make new choices that affect our feelings and influence our attitudes. We can also be more educated and open minded about subjects which can lead to developing new and positive attitudes.

Here's a quote that you can take to the bank:

"You can change your life by changing your attitude!"
—Author unknown

(Keep in mind that the only one who likes change is a wet baby!)

28

PERCEPTION 101

The second half in the equation of stress is perception. Perception is how we personally process and interpret the events in our lives. The main reason some people cope better with stress than others has to do, to some extent, with perception. How you perceive or view a situation is everything. It is not the situation that generates your stress, it is the meaning you place on the situation! If you say to yourself, "This is the worst thing that's ever happened to me. I will never overcome it." Chances are, you won't, and you will be scarred for life. However, if you say "This is the worst thing that's ever happened to me, but I will survive it!" It is more likely you will eventually find a way to accept the terrible event, get on with your life, and most likely become stronger from it.

A prime example of using such a coping strategy can be learned from studying some Vietnam Veterans who were held captive during the war. A study showed many POW's were exposed to the hardship of captivity; yet they still emerged emotionally stable. They achieved this by altering their perception of their situation. Where most would only see darkness, by adopting a positive coping strategy, they managed to find light. One major cause of stress is the combination of high responsibility and low control. Many of the POW's felt a sense of high responsibility to help their fellow comrades make it through the ordeal. No matter how bad things got for the POW's, they could still control their thoughts by focusing on the good or positive, such as the days they received food, or were not beaten. Keep in mind that while you can't control everything life throws your way, by adjusting your perceptions about stressful situations, you can reclaim a lot of control over the duration of stressful experiences.

PERCEPTION EXERCISE – THE ELEPHANT

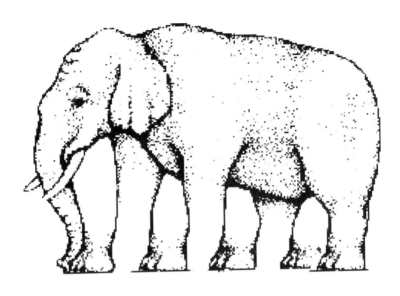

How many legs does the Elephant have?

In the optical illusion of the elephant, most people will see more than four legs. We all know, however, that elephants only have four legs. This exercise demonstrates that what one focuses on, can become one's perceived reality! So, maybe there is NO reality, only perception. If you look for beauty, you will find beauty. If you look for conspiracies, you will find conspiracies. If you have a hammer, then everything looks like a nail. However, the same hammer that shatters the glass also forges the steel.

"What we see depends mainly on what we look for"
—John Lubborck

IT DEPENDS ON HOW YOU LOOK AT IT

(A story adapted with permission from PositiveChristianity.org)

A man pulled into a gas station on the outskirts of town. As he filled his tank, he remarked to the attendant, "I've just accepted a job in town. I've never been to this part of the country. What are people like here?" "What are people like where you came from?" the attendant asked. "Not so nice," the man replied. "In fact, they can be quite rude." The attendant shook his head, "Well, I'm afraid you'll find the people in this town to be the same way."

Just then another car pulled into the station. "Excuse me," the driver called out. "I'm just moving to this area. Is it nice here?" "Was it nice where you came from?" the attendant inquired. "Oh, yes! I came from a great place. The people were friendly, and I hated to leave." "Well, you'll find the same to be true of this town." "Thanks!" yelled the driver as he pulled away. "So what is this town really like?" asked the first man, now irritated with the attendant's conflicting reports. The attendant just shrugged his shoulders. "It's all a matter of perception. You'll find things to be just the way you think they are."

In everyday life there are a multitude of problems, each one causing a different level of stress. Look again at your problem with a different perception. Now that you have looked at it, does your problem, the root of your stress, seem to be worse than it really is, or is there really a problem at all? In many ways the experience of emotional stress is quite self-inflicted and your attitudes and perceptions play a big role.

STRESS LESS

Is stress always bad for you? Can zero stress make you happy and healthy? The answer to both questions is, No! To begin with, some stress is helpful! Without stress, we would have little motivation to do things, like get out of bed to go to work on Monday morning. Some first responders even claim to "do their best work under stress," stating that it heightens their alertness, focuses their attention on the task at hand, and improves their performance overall. But, stress is only good in small amounts. Think of stress to the human body as compared to the tension on violin strings: too little tension and the music is dull and raspy; too much, and the music is shrill or the strings snap. A common method for preventing stress overload is to train first responders to recognize the sources and signs of it and to develop individual strategies for coping with it. By developing individual strategies, one can learn to balance out the stress in his or her life and "stress less." The term "stress less" is not a vague term without meaning or thought. Quite the contrary, the term has a profound meaning in that it refers to:

- Being prepared for stress
- Increasing your tolerance to stress
- Practicing stress-minimizing activities on a daily basis

BEING PREPARED FOR STRESS

If you were to ask a group of people to write down things which cause stress in their lives, you would see problems common to most and a definite stress pattern. The pattern can be generalized into 10 categories of stress. (This may not be a very scientific survey, but, it is sure a lot cheaper than having the government compile a $3,000,000 study at tax payer's expense just to come up with the same results.)

THE TEN NON-SCIENTIFIC CATEGORIES OF STRESS:

1. Employment (layoffs, inadequate pay, reduced benefits)
2. Money (debt, paying for college, braces, alimony)
3. Traffic (traffic jams, rude drivers, traffic collisions)
4. Taxes (property tax & income tax)
5. Illness or injury (personal, family or friends)
6. Death (not your own but someone you know or an influential figure like JFK)
7. Family Issues (new baby, problems with the out-laws (in-laws), a child leaving home for the first time to go into college, the military or jail!)
8. Natural Disasters (hurricane, floods, earthquakes, fires, and tornados)
9. Crime (against person or property, terrorism)
10. Too many sacrifices (time for your spouse, kids, and employer and not enough time for yourself)

We are sure that if you were to take a moment and write down the things that cause stress in your life, that it could be filed into one of the categories listed above. (If you can't fit some of your stresses into those main categories you might want to immediately seek professional help or call *Ripley's Believe it or Not.*) Most of the stressors in the above categories are predictable, and thus, can be prepared for or prevented. For example, if you have to travel on a highway route that is well-known for being extremely congested, your slow commute, and the stress involved, is predictable. Knowing this information in advance can give you an opportunity to stress less by preparing to do such things as: leave a little earlier, take an alternative route, bring a favorite CD or maybe just a book on tape. The same formula could be applied to the other categories of stress such as illness or injury. Whereas you may not be able to predict when an illness or injury might befall you or a loved one, especially in the dangerous occupation of first responders,

there are simple preparatory steps you can take to reduce the stress involved. Some preliminary steps include: having adequate medical insurance, disability insurance, durable power of medical attorney, a will or trust, and adequate savings to help reduce the strain of medical costs or lost wages. Being prepared will help you cope better to the unpredictable circumstances and therefore help diminish the stress.

INCREASING YOUR TOLERANCE TO STRESS

The word 'tolerance' means; "the ability to endure or resist the harmful effects of." As we already know, a problem situation is a stressful situation. To increase your tolerance to a problem situation you must first determine your connection to the problem. Sometimes other people's problems can cause you harmful effects too. First responders, in an attempt to be helpful, sometimes see it as their mission to manage other people's stress and relieve all it's symptoms. Not only is this a heavy stress burden to bear, but it will also set you up for failure. By learning to develop realistic expectations of yourself and others, you can help change your reactions and approach to problem situations, which in turn will help you stress less.

"I can't change the world, but I can change one thing at a time."
– Thomas Bremer

Another way for first responders to endure the harmful effects of stress is to keep in mind that you can't always solve a problem situation. This is not to say, however, that you can't at least fix some of it. It is also true that as first responders we can't always find a solution that will make everyone happy. As soon as you realize these truths; that there is no perfect solution and sometimes you can only solve little pieces of a problem at a time, you begin making progress towards increasing your tolerance to stress!

THE DONKEY FABLE:

An old man, a boy and a donkey were going to town. The boy rode on the donkey and the old man walked. As they went along, they passed some people who remarked that it was a shame the old man was walking and the boy was riding. The man and boy thought maybe the critics were right, so they changed positions.

Later, they passed some people that remarked, "What a shame, he makes that little boy walk." They then decided they both would walk! Soon they passed some more people who thought they were stupid to walk when they had a decent donkey to ride. So, they both rode the donkey.

Now they passed some people that shamed them by saying how awful to put such a load on a poor donkey. The boy and man said they were probably right, so they decided to carry the donkey. As they crossed the bridge, they lost their grip on the animal and he fell into the river and drowned.

The Moral of the story: If you try to please everyone, you might as well kiss your ass good-bye.

"I don't know the key to success
but the key to failure is to try to please everyone"
—Bill Cosby

PRACTICE STRESS
MINIMIZING ACTIVITIES ON A DAILY BASIS

The first step towards balancing your stress is to learn how to recognize the signs of stress. The second is to take steps to replenish and care for yourself by adopting new lifestyle habits. This will increase your emotional resiliency, allowing you to "fight back" against the stress."

IDEAS TO STRESS LESS

HAVE PERSONAL RESOURCES

Everyone needs a strong social support network. This can be accomplished by developing a personal community filled with family, friends, clergy, professional counselors, trained peer support, and colleagues. People from this community are in the best position to recognize your own unique signs of stress. This support group is more likely to tell you when you look like hell and seem overwhelmed. Their honest reflections can help you recognize when your adaptation capacity has reached its limits. Plus, another person can help you see your problem in a new light or from a different perspective. They can offer help, or guide you towards professional help. Having someone in place that you feel comfortable expressing your own thoughts, feelings and opinions with can help diminish your stressful reactions that would otherwise continue to build. These people, however, are of little use if you don't talk to them when you are feeling stressed and out of balance. Get over the reluctance to ask for help. Remember, no one achieves personal or professional success without the help of others.

"One good reason for maintaining only a small circle of friends is that three out of four murders are committed by people who know the victim."
—George Carlin

INCORPORATE A BALANCED DIET

Comfort eating is a common reaction to stress, and during a stressful period, people are more inclined to eat unhealthy. During a time of stress, most people begin to crave carbohydrates. This is because carbohydrates boost serotonin, a brain chemical that has a calming effect. The human body, however, metabolizes all carbohydrates into sugar, leading to a roller coaster of highs and lows. Carbohydrates come in two forms; simplex and complex. Examples of simplex forms are: white bread, white rice, and most junk foods. During times of stress when cravings are inclined to increase, skip the candy and sugar and opt instead for the high-quality, complex carbs such as whole grain breads, cereals, and starchy vegetables. Many nutritional experts differ on the definition of a balanced or proper diet. All, however, agree people need to eat more complex carbs instead of simple carbs. Proper nutrition is essential for a happy life. "Junk food is our enemy!" A balanced and proper diet can also help you avoid disorders such as heart disease, diabetes, obesity, hypertension, and many types of cancers.

AVOID CHEMICAL FIXES

Using alcohol to relax, sleeping pills to sleep or other types of medication to cope with stress will not reduce stress in the long run. These types of chemical fixes can lead to dependency, adding a host of new problems and stressors to your daily life. Chemical intake impairs one's judgment and ability to truly cope with stress.

LISTEN TO MUSIC

It is true, music soothes the savage beast, and it also works wonders for first responders. Studies have shown that listening to music can provide a calming and positive affect on our emotions and creativity. With the introduction of new electronic devices, the ability to listen to music on the go has never been easier. So, when stressed out; "Rock Out!"

GET REGULAR PHYSICAL EXERCISE

First responders work in a high pressure environment making proper exercise vital to their stress management. Exercise is a great way to counter stress stored in your body and provide an outlet for the residual tension created by the fight-or-flight response. It can help you work out the tension in your muscles and your mind, helping you to relax and sleep better. One study has shown that 60% of clinically depressed people who took a brisk thirty minute walk or jog at least three times a week were no longer depressed after sixteen weeks. Add movement to your life such as dancing, walking, running, and stretching. Movement is essential for optimal health; however, remember to stay away from climbing the walls, pushing your luck or running in circles.

TAKE RECESS TIME AT WORK

A recent study found that nearly one-third of employees work through lunch and never leave the building once they arrive for work. Nineteen percent said they felt obligated to work, even when sick or injured. Consider getting away from your hectic schedule at work by taking a 5-10 minute "mini vacation." This short break can help you put things into perspective and help restore your energy.

38

Then, when you return to your work, you will do so with a more positive attitude and a more relaxed feeling. For first responders who work in an indoor environment, such as a desk job or dispatcher, they need to take a break from their closed surroundings by going outside and breathing some fresh air. . .unless you live in a big, smoggy city. Don't work yourself to death!

GET A HOBBY

Balance out the stress in your life by developing a hobby to which you can apply your imagination. Having a hobby or passion for something outside of work can provide a calming sense of control, overall serenity, and can also lower blood pressure. Plus, many hobbies are social, giving you much needed positive human contact.

ANIMALS

Whereas some people see pets as an additional source of stress, the fact is, companion animals are a proven form of stress management. Pet therapy is frequently used in hospitals and nursing homes to increase socialization and to reduce depression, anger and stress. Many people feel more relaxed when their pets are present. Pets such as dogs and cats provide unconditional, nonjudgmental love and affection. After a hard day at work, this kind of interaction can really help you to calm down and relax. Finally, if you have a dog as a pet, most likely it will be taking you on a walk on a daily basis. This will afford you some exercise, fresh air, time to collect your thoughts or daydream, and the perfect excuse to take time for yourself, away from your stressors. There is some truth in the saying that, "dogs are man's best friend!"

MAKE YOURSELF A PRIORITY

Make more time for yourself daily. Take an eight hour lunch break once in a while. This "Me time" is crucial to help you think and put things in perspective, and necessary for your own well being. It will

also have a direct positive impact on those around you! Keep in mind the "Airplane Rule." This is the instructions given to passengers before take-off, telling the adults in case of an emergency to first put the oxygen mask on themselves before they put a mask on their child. This rule demonstrates that you must make yourself a priority and take care of your needs first. If you don't, you might not have what it takes to help others. Budget your time wisely by writing a to-do list for the next day. On the list, make your needs a high priority. Also, allow for breaks or time that you do nothing at all but think. There will always be one more thing to do, but when people don't take time out for themselves, they stop being productive.

Use Positive Self-Talk

Everyday we have many personal conversations with ourselves, most of which involves negative thinking. Even in conversations with others about yourself, negative self-talk is prevalent. All of this creates personal stress on the mind and body. You don't need to listen to your own poisonous messages. You don't need to be victimized by your own thoughts. Rather than berate and belittle yourself for any shortcoming, try repeating positive affirmations to yourself such as:

"I am a creative individual and am capable of seeing my way through this."

"This setback is only temporary, and I will rebound even stronger!"

"I am open to new opportunities."

"Something good is going to come of this!"

Even in the face of failure or a serious problem, the use of encouraging, positive self-talk will fortify your spirit, strengthen your ego, help you move forward, and restore balance in your life. Practice positive thinking and it will become automatic. Optimism is a habit of thinking. Look for the silver linings in each black cloud.

"THE SANDS OF TIME"

A professor stood before her Philosophy 101 class and had some items in front of her. When the class began, wordlessly, she picked up a very large and empty mayonnaise jar and proceeded to fill it with golf balls. She then asked the students if the jar was full. They agreed that it was. So the professor then picked up a box of pebbles and poured them into the jar. She shook the jar lightly. The pebbles, of course rolled into the open areas between the golf balls. She then asked the students if the jar was full. They agreed it was. The professor picked up a box of sand and poured it into the jar. Of course, the sand filled up everything else. She then asked once more if the jar was full. The students responded with a unanimous-yes. The professor then produced two cans of liquid chocolate from under the table and proceeded to pour the contents into the jar effectively filling the empty space between the sand. The students laughed.

"Now," said the professor, "This jar represents your life. The golf balls are the important things; your family, your spouse, your health, your children, your friends, your favorite passions—things that if everything else was lost and only they remained, your life would still be full.

"The pebbles are the other things like your job, your house, your car. The sand is everything else—the small stuff."

"If you put sand in the jar first," she continued, "there is no room for the pebbles or the golf balls. The same goes for your life. If you spend all your time and energy on the small stuff, you will never have room for the things that are important to you. Pay attention to the things that are critical to your happiness. Play with your children and grandchildren. Take time to get medical checkups. Take your partner out dancing. Take riding lessons. There will always be time to go to work, clean the house, give a dinner party and fix the garbage disposal."

"Take care of the golf balls first, the things that really matter. Set your priorities. The rest is just sand." One of the students raised her hand and inquired what the chocolate represented. The professor smiled. "I'm glad you asked. It just goes to show you that no matter how full your life may seem, there's always room for chocolate!"

41

STOP, JOT AND GOAL

In order to be content in your life, you need direction, you need an itinerary, and you need a map. You probably wouldn't drive from Los Angeles to New York without a map. GOALS are your road map to life! The trouble with not having goals is that you spend your entire life driving around in circles, eventually running out of gas. Goals are one of those things that make your life better. Having goals helps you to clarify what is important to you in life. Successful people always have clear and focused goals that guide them. Setting goals has other benefits too, such as:

- Clear and focused thoughts, actions and direction
- Maximizes use of time
- High enthusiasm

People that use goals effectively suffer less stress, show more self-confidence, and are happier and more satisfied. "Now" is a good time to stop, jot and goal. Take some time to really think about what you want out of your life and the direction you want to go. Jot these ideas down on a piece of paper. Seeing the goals written down will help clarify what is important to you in life, and will then help you take the next step in turning your thoughts and dreams into reality. If you don't firmly choose the course you will follow, the relentless drift of events will make the decision for you.

*"You've got to be very careful if you don't know
where you are going, because you might not get there."*
—Yogi Berra

SET LIMITS

"Just say no" is an essential tool in caring for yourself. Setting definite parameters can free you up to say "no" to requests that don't align with your schedule or vision, without feeling guilt. On the other hand, it is sometimes okay to say "yes," when people ask if they can help you. As first responders, we are in the business of helping others, but sometimes, it is okay to allow others to help you. Remember, unless you have a big "S" on your red under suit, you aren't Superman.

GET ENOUGH OF SLEEP.

Too little sleep will make any adult act like a tall two-year old. Getting an inadequate amount of sleep will take its toll on your motivation, energy, and attitude. Adequate sleep allows you to better cope with stress. Some people can get by on six hours of sleep each night, while others need 7-8 hours. Regardless of how many hours you require, make sure you get enough sleep. You'll be more likely to wake up with a smile and with energy. Life is short and if you are to make the most out of everyday you need to get proper sleep.

PROBLEM SOLVING

For some people, life hasn't begun, or it has taken a back seat, because of the problems in their life. There will always be some obstacle in the way, something to be gotten through first, some unfinished business, or a debt to be paid. Don't let problems make you wait for life to begin. These obstacles are life. Sometimes it takes a crisis or problem to find out who you are, what you stand for, or what you stand against. Look at problems logically. Simply look at any stressful situation, problem, conflict, struggle or intense emotional experience, and ask yourself, "Am I reacting to fact or fiction?" When you let emotions take over, you may do something that makes sense at the time, but in the end wasn't the best choice. Don't overreact, instead, ask yourself, how can I prevent this from happening again, and how can I learn from this? Life is full of obstacle illusions. Take action and get on with life!

43

Journal for Your Health

Writing has long been known as good therapy, providing a positive effect on overall health. Keeping a journal is like having a heart-to-heart talk with yourself. Studies have shown that people who keep a personal journal and regularly write about their emotions, suffer less anxiety and depression. Have a notebook and pen handy at all times to jot down what you are thinking and feeling when faced with a problem. Note how often you use words such as blame, guilt, anger, and despair. Journaling can be a great problem solving tool and is a positive way to manage your emotions rather than ignoring them. In addition, this is a great way for first responders to capsulate their career.

Obtain Solitude

In today's world, first responders are bombarded with an over abundance of external stimulation. The human body was not design to handle such a large amount of stimuli. Overwhelmed by such distractions, people become more irritable, causing a decreased ability to concentrate, thus making their mind feel more muddled and their problems more imposing than they actually are. Solitude is a way to escape the chaos and a necessary tool to recharge your batteries in a way that sleep can't. Sleep restores us physically, while solitude restores our psyche. Solitude is not just about being physically alone; it's also about having only yourself on the agenda. Solitude can provide you the time to deal with your feelings and confront your problems without being influenced by outside distractions. Find a nice, quiet place and relax. For a short period of time, lose the technology such as cell phones, pagers, and laptops. It can be very stressful being plugged into the world and being available to others at all times. The reduction of unnecessary stimulation will allow for a deeper state of the relaxation, helping you find inspiration, clarity, focus, and inner balance. Living a balanced life requires that you take time for self-reflection in order to identify what's important to you. Solitude is an antidote to the super speed we live.

8 STEPS TO STRESS MANAGEMENT THROUGH VISUALIZATION

1) Picture yourself near a stream.
2) Birds are softly chirping in the cool mountain air.
3) No one but you knows your secret place.
4) You are in total seclusion from the hectic place called, "the world."
5) The soothing sound of a gentle waterfall fills the air with a cascade of serenity.
6) The water is crystal clear.
7) You can easily make out the face of the person you're holding underwater.
8) See, you're smiling already!

CREATE A STRESS LESS ENVIRONMENTAL

Experts say we are creatures of our own environment, and sometimes this environment causes us discomfort and stress. It is safe to say if we improve our surroundings, we can improve our life. Here are several tips to help you achieve a stress-less environment:

• Improve air quality in your home and office by banning smoking, opening windows, and introducing plants where air is dry. Plants will help raise the humidity in the air, improve oxygenation, and help absorb unpleasant odors. Improve illumination. Bright light and/or poor lightning in your environment can cause you eye strain and increased fatigue.

• Clean your way to a stress-less environment. An environment that is dirty can cause stress. Physical clutter can easily lead to mental clutter. Keep your life organized and you will find more energy and clarity in your life. Assign places to store commonly used items, such as your keys, purse, briefcase, tools, clothing, and accessories. A good rule of thumb when it comes to organizing is, if you haven't used it in 6 months, get rid of it!

- This is a loud, loud world. Noise can cause intense stress. Reduce the noise in your life by installing partitions to deaden sound, separate meeting rooms, have a quiet room for homework, relaxing, working, or just thinking. To escape the noise, try playing a blank tape at full volume.

- Straighten your life out through good ergonomics. Poorly designed furniture can cause muscular tension and pain. Investing in a good chair, back/lumbar support, and a keyboard wrist support will be of great physical benefit to you. Plus, it's a good tax write off.

(Consult your tax adviser before using)

FAST FACT

Bad back? Physical therapy and/or prescribed excercises may help stabilize your spine, build your endurance, and increase your flexibility.

DO THE RIGHT THING

As a society, we know bad people do the wrong things, and good people do the right things. First responders pride themselves on doing the right things. Doing the right thing, however, sometimes goes way beyond mere legal compliance. Many things that are not illegal, such as taking advantage of trust, are unethical. It is essential to determine whether an action is truly right and not just a rationalized self-interest. Doing the right thing really means contributing to the general good and avoiding consequences that hurt others. For example, say you are driving down the road. Everything is going fine when you notice the car ahead of you in the other lane activate his turn signal. This action is notifying you that he wants to merge into your lane. You are now faced with two choices. One, speed up and not allow him to merge in front of you, or two, allow the car to merge. This first action has a high probability of causing you stress when the driver of the other car honks at you and gives you the one finger wave. A less stressful solution is to slow down, allow the car to merge in front of you and feel good about your act of courtesy. In the end, you can't go wrong by doing what you know is right.

THE PATH TO GOOD KARMA:

- Always be truthful
- Display acts of kindness
- Be just to everyone

TRIAD OF BALANCE

"Balance = Whole Life, not a Hole Life!"

The dictionary definition of "balance" is: mental or emotional stability; a state of equilibrium. Balance is everywhere; from nature, to our government's constitutional systems of checks and balances. Balance is important in every aspect of life; from balancing the tires on your car, eating a balanced diet, to balancing you checkbook. Even your body maintains balance through the process of homeostasis. By shifting fluids and chemicals throughout the cells, the body is able to maintain a balanced environment.

JOKE

A man walked into a bank. As he approached a teller window, he tripped. Fortunately, he caught himself before he fell. The teller watching his acrobatic act jokingly commented to him, *"Apparently, sir. You came here to get your balance."*

Now, you've probably heard experts talk about "life balance." So, what does that really mean? A good definition of "life balance" is having a clear vision about what you want out of life with defined priorities. This will clarify what is important in your life. The process of balance, or the outcome, is to live life to the fullest! Life balance is a daily blend of life, work, and relationships that equates to a well-rounded, balanced lifestyle. Life balance consists of the following seven vital areas:

- Health
- Family
- Social
- Financial
- Professional
- Spiritual
- Intellectual

By spending sufficient quality time on a daily basis in each of these areas, you will have a balanced life. Ignore one or more of these areas and you go out of balance. For example; fail to spend time now on your health, and you may develop an illness later on. Ignoring your spouse could cost you a lot of time in the future, repairing the relationship, or even cost you a divorce. Now is the time to make balance vital in your life. Too many people deceive themselves into thinking there will be time later to enjoy the fruits of their labor. They ignorantly put off time with their families, hobbies, spiritual development and health maintenance. Don't wait! There are no guarantees in life, and living a full and balanced life should not be postponed!

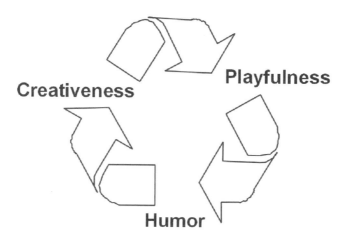

The living of life, even a balanced life, creates stress! The simple truth is that something is not stressful unless we allow it to be. The foundation for stress is always your attitude and perception. The "Triad of Balance" is a formula consisting of creativity, humor, and playfulness. This "Triad" helps you to take a stressful situation and redefine it. This will allow you to cope or balance out the everyday stresses in your life. Whereas the "Triad of Balance" is a strong stress management strategy, a great idea, and a foundation to help you deal with the stress in your life, it isn't always a substitute for professional help needed to deal with a stress

problem. By using the "Triad of Balance," it will help you to improve your ability to cope with stress and deal with it, before it deals with you in the form of injury or disease. In the "Triad" formula, the three points: creativity, humor, and playfulness are all closely related. Developing skills in creativity will help you find humor, and appreciating a wide variety of humor will help develop your creativity. Humor means having fun, and creativity requires a good dose of fun and play. Most of all, the "Triad" is the antidote to the common adult health condition: Seriousitis. This disease has infected millions of professional adults, resulting in the somber and severe condition of being too serious. Whereas most adults think the business of living life needs to be a serious one, and in some aspects it should, the bottom line is that living too seriously is a dangerous shift away from some of the main aspects that make life enjoyable. By implementing the "Triad" into your life, it may seem that you are playing the fool, however, in this instance, that is exactly what you want to be — a F.O.O.L., which really means: <u>F</u>ull <u>O</u>peration <u>O</u>f <u>L</u>ife! Having full operation of your life will help you discover the parts that have been missing, allowing you to achieve happiness.

CREATIVENESS

"The Only Truly Happy People Are Children
And The Creative Minority!"
—Jean Caldwell

Experts believe that we think 60,000 thoughts a day, but 90% of those thoughts are repeats. You don't have to be a Rocket Scientist to figure out we're only using 10% of our creativity.

SPOT EXPERIMENT:

In the following experiment, a number of adults were gathered in a room and told to sit on a couch. An instructor then came in, removed a white piece of paper from a desk and drew a small, dime-sized black spot in it.

The instructor then asked the adults what it was. After a few moments of deep contemplation, the consensus of the group was that it resembled a small, dark spot! WOW, what creative thinkers! Immediately after this eye-opening experiment, the instructor decided to try it again, but this time he would attempt the same experiment with children. So, in came the kids, and again he drew a small, dark spot on a white sheet of paper and asked them what it was. Within seconds, the kids started shouting out their surprisingly different answers. The kids said the spot looked like; an owls eye, a star, a pebble, a squashed bug. One even said it looked like a butt without the crack!"

Psychology studies show that 90% of all five-year olds are creative! However, only 10% of all 7 year olds are creative. Sadly, only 2% of all persons age 8-45 still have significant creative juices flowing.

There are two main reasons we aren't more creative. The first reason is that we are taught early on to be logical, and to look for the "right answer". Like robots, we follow the programming taught to us. The second reason why we aren't more creative is that we don't need to be. We are creatures of habit when it comes to the business of living. Though routines are indispensable, and without them our lives would be in chaos, they also reduce the need for creativity. Take for example, a daily commute to work. Everyday you drive the same exact route, never varying from your pre-determined course. Taking this route, you would always arrive at the same place, at the same time, never varying your level of stimulus. If one day, however, you were to try a street you had never been down before, you might find it to be a quicker, and maybe a more enjoyable way to go. So, if you are looking to improve your life, or to stress less, you must start thinking <u>differently</u> or <u>creatively</u>!

"The definition of insanity is doing things the same way and expecting different results."
—Benjamin Franklin

BENEFITS OF CREATIVITY:

- Creative thinking will help you out from under the influence of attitudes!
- Creative thinking stretches the border of our usual and practical thinking!
- Creative jolts in your routine can lead you to new ideas.
- Creative tasks are deeply absorbing and satisfying.
- Creative tasks distract you from everyday pressures, anxieties, and stress.

"In an interaction with limits, the first responder will benefit tremendously when the creative act comes into play!"
—Dan Jordan, First Responder & Magician

HOW TO BE CRE8TIVE AGAIN

Change Your Routine Thinking

General George Patton once said, "If everyone is thinking alike then someone isn't thinking!" How true is that! Creative thinking requires an outlook that breaks routine thinking by searching for ideas and playing with your knowledge and experience. Do you do things because that's the way it's always been done? If so, you might be too practical and non-creative. You can't be creative if you're always being practical, following the program, afraid to make mistakes or look foolish by coming up with unusual ideas. Discovery/creativity consists of looking at the same thing as everyone else and thinking something different. Give yourself permission to be creative and break your routine habits. When things change and new information comes into existence, it forces creative abilities to find new answers, new solutions and new ideas to existing problems or stresses. This will lead to new ideas and successes, and will help you to stress less!

CRE8TIVE EXERCISE #1- THE MAZE

INSTRUCTIONS: Using a pencil, draw the quickest path from the start of the maze to the finish. Time yourself to see how long it takes.

Are you done? How long did it take to solve this problem? If you are like most people, it took you thirty seconds to two minutes to draw a line through the twisting maze. You could have, however, completed it within two seconds. Maybe you were focusing on the wrong thing. You could have easily drawn a curved line around the outside of the maze from the start to finish and it isn't against the rules. Nothing in the rules stated to stay within the maze. But, because you have probably followed the logical path engrained in you at an early age on how to do mazes, you assumed that you should draw a twisting line through the maze. Most likely, you fell into the trap of conventional thinking and focused on the wrong thing, therefore missing the *quickest path from start to finish.*

BE CHILDLIKE

Another way to increase your creativity is to question things just like kids do. In other words, be open minded and curious, be childlike but not childish. Ask why and see what new thoughts this provokes.

- Why do hot-dogs come in packages of 8 and buns in packages of 10?
- Why do we drive in parkways and park in driveways?
- Why isn't there mouse flavored cat food?
- Why does Goofy stand erect while Pluto remains on all fours? They're both dogs!
- Why does someone believe you when you say there are four billion stars, but check when you say the paint is wet?
- Why do they report power outages on TV?
- Why does Superman stop bullets with his chest, but ducks when someone throws a gun at him?
- Why do they lock gas station bathrooms? Are they afraid someone will clean them?!
- The guy on the wanted poster....Why didn't the police just hold him when they took the picture?

Question: What ingredients are in a peanut butter and jelly sandwich?

As a child, our minds are like a clean slate, willing and able to be creative. Given the task of making his own sandwich, a child may create his own version of a peanut butter and jelly sandwich using different ingredients that may go against a logical adult's thinking. This is because it is customary for adults to think in terms of logical connections. By breaking out of this reasoning, changing the question, and thinking in terms of "what if," you can increase your creativity.

What if men could become pregnant?
What if cars were fueled with food?
What if animals were smarter than people?

"The curiosity that we can all have in ourselves and develop in ourselves is the only thing that can really lead us to creativity!"
—Daniel Barenboim

CRE8TIVE EXERCISE # 2 – NEWSPAPER CHALLENGE

INSTRUCTIONS: Can you think of a way in which you can put a sheet of newspaper on the floor so that when two people stand face to face on it, they won't be able to touch one another?

* Cutting or tearing the paper is not allowed and neither is tying up the people or preventing them from moving.

ANSWER: For answer, hold page up to mirror!

Begin today to rediscover cre8tivity in your life. Start by taking small steps such as listening to music that's not familiar to you, trying a new seating arrangement at the dinner table, or even eating your desserts first. (Desserts is Stressed spelled backwards.) If you read the newspaper, try reading the funny pages first, and then read into the silly headlines like the ones below:

- *"Judge to rule on nude beach!"*
- *"Police step up effort to run down jaywalkers!"*
- *"Jurors are hung in the Peterson case!"*

The best way to get a good idea is to get a lot of ideas! Creativity can help you find new ideas and ways to improve your life and stress less. Remember, problems are stress, being creative with your problems may reduce your stress. No problem is bigger than one person armed with creativity and the will to use it! Believe in yourself and be a creative risk taker and you might just be rewarded for taking a leap of faith with an imaginative idea! Even simple creative jolts in your routine can lead you to new ideas and successes!

"You can't use up creativity.
The more you use, the more you have."
—Maya Angelou

PLAYFULNESS

"All men die, but not all men live!"
-Author unknown

Playfulness is the second part in the "Triad of Balance." Playfulness is the ability to act silly, and not take yourself so seriously. In other words, "Lighten Up!" By being playful, you give yourself a license to try different approaches in life, without the fear of penalties.

"Having fun is not a diversion
from a successful life; it is a pathway to it."
—Oprah Winfrey

BENEFITS OF PLAYFULNESS:

- Playfulness is an integral part of personal and professional success.
- A sense of playfulness is an important ingredient in job satisfaction!
- You, and your organization, can play and still have your eyes closely fixed on the bottom line.
- Play breeds creativity. Creativity breeds new ideas, new products, and new successes.
- A playful attitude is fundamental to creative thinking because your defenses are down, your attitude is loosened, and there is little concern with rules, practicality, or being wrong.
- A light and playful attitude stimulates creative thoughts which can actually increase productivity!

"I never did a day of work in my life. It was all fun."
-Thomas Edison

The essence of playfulness is exploring, and exploring means; to travel in a region previously unknown to educate one self about its natural features, inhabitants or to examine carefully; look into closely, investigate. Children naturally are explorers and have a simple way of looking at things, making life fun for them. This is something serious professional adults can benefit from. As serious adults we don't take the time out of our regular daily lives to get out and explore our surroundings. This fact greatly minimizes our exposure to fun.

As adults, one exciting way we do explore and have fun is by vacationing. Our vacations often take us to fun and exotic places. One of the most popular vacation spots in the United States is Las Vegas. We're guessing that, based on their extremely memorable slogan, *"What happens in Vegas, stays in Vegas,"* people do become very playful on vacation. So maybe the answer to becoming more playful, is to take more vacations, or at least live your life as if everyday is a vacation.

Most supervisors won't agree with that theory, but then again they are usually very serious people! Being playful and having fun helps balance out your serious life! Fun and play are not always what we make happen, but what we allow to happen. By allowing yourself to be more playful, it will help you to start living life to its fullest and not stress or worry about the little things or matters over which you have little or no control. A benefit to taking the time to be playful and living everyday like it is a vacation is that it allows you to replace some of the serious time in your life, reducing your stress, and putting things in proper perspective. But, even though vacationing is one way to be more playful and have more fun, taking a working vacation is not the answer. In fact, a "working vacation" is an oxymoron.

OTHER OXYMORON'S:

Jumbo Shrimp / Found Missing / Resident Alien / Legally Drunk / Sports Sedan / Silent Alarm / Diet Ice-cream / Airline Food / Peace-Keeper Missile / Dry Lake / Forward Lateral / Civil War / Government Organization

"Look at me, look at me,
Look at me now.
It is fun to have fun,
But you have to know how."
—Dr. Seuss

Positive Key Aspects of Play:
- Imagination
- Self-confidence/self-esteem
- Creativity
- Problem solving
- Cooperation
- Balance
- Exploring

Do you feel something's missing in your life? Go back to something you once loved, but left. In the exercise below, write down things you use to do for fun but aren't doing now. (If you are married don't write down, "dating," not funny!) By doing this exercise, you will rediscover a precious piece of yourself that got buried with time, responsibility, and seriousness.

1. _____
2. _____
3. _____
4. _____
5. _____

HUMOR

"With the fearful strain that is on me night and day,
if I did not laugh I should die."
—Abraham Lincoln

Humor is the third and final part in the "Triad of Balance." Psychological research has found that a person's sense of humor is associated with intelligence, creativity, positive self-concepts and leadership in business. Humor, though, is something not usually found in the work place. The fact is we spend a majority of our time and life at work. Once established in a career, professional people tend to suffer from Seriousitis, which can be terminally grave to their personality. Some people relate professionalism to being serious which in reality hurts creativity, energy, spirit, and authentic self. A sense of humor is an attitude, willingness and intention to see the non-serious element(s) in a serious situation. Humor gives us the opportunity to take ourselves less seriously. Studies show that employers value a person with a sense of humor. In a poll done by Hodge-Cronin of 1,000 bosses, 98% said they preferred hiring an applicant with a good sense of humor. In the same poll, 84% believed that people with a sense of humor would do a better job.

"The less confident you are, the more serious you have to act"
—Tara Ploughman

With an about-face, this person takes humor seriously

This person suffers from seriousitis!

NOTE: *The typical child laughs 400 times a day, but adults laugh only about 15!*

QUESTION: Why should we laugh at work?
ANSWER: Humor is important because people are important!

The profession of being a first responder is very stressful. When you are under stress, your sense of humor is one of the first things to go! But, if you can laugh at the situation and yourself, you'll be amazed at how much better you feel. A sense of humor doesn't necessarily mean a knack for telling jokes. Rather, it means the ability to shift your perspective in order to take some setbacks and still see that the world has not come to an end. Keep in mind that if all you do in a crisis is add to the mess and confusion, people and fellow workers will soon lose respect for your abilities under pressure. If you can maintain your sense of perspective and humor when the world seems to be falling apart, people who rely on you will show their appreciation in better work and greater loyalty. Yes, some problems and situations a first responder

faces are serious, however, there is nothing to be gained by exaggerating their importance. Get in the habit of taking yourself and your problems less seriously. Humor makes every situation a first responder faces more bearable. Anything that can help you take your job seriously, but yourself lightly is good. A prime example of this is the humorous stories found in the second half of this book.

THE FUNCTIONS OF HUMOR:

Emotionally
1. Acts as a coping mechanism to help one better face life's problems and is a healthy escape from reality.
2. Relieves stress and anxiety, and releases emotions such as anger and guilt.
3. Prevents tension. So, women, humor is the best cosmetic!
4. Helps you find your PMA; Positive Mental Attitude.

Socially
1. Lessens the hierarchy between individuals.
2. Establishes rapport.
3. Opens the door for communication.
4. Helps convey information.
5. Solidifies a group.
6. Neutralizes highly emotional events.

"A smile is the shortest distance between two people!"
—Victor Borge

Physically
1. Increases respiration and oxygen exchange. (belly laughter – air in / air out like internal jogging)
2. Laughter has been shown to lower rates of allergies and infections.
3. Activates and strengthens your immune system.

4. Reduces the risk of heart disease.
5. Helps with digestion and sleep.
6. After attending a laughter session (comedy movie) partici-
   pants have lower blood pressure and fewer complaints about
   aches or pains.

Humor is also the best medicine,
unless you're really sick,
then call 9-1-1

HUMOR SAFETY

As with anything, it is easy to abuse a good thing and humor is NO exception. There is only two ways to use humor – appropriately and inappropriately.

"Humor is laughter made from pain, not pain inflicted by laughter."
—Joel Goodman

Inappropriate humor is negative and destructive humor. It lowers self-esteem, belittles and excludes others, creates tension, targets laughter at someone such as a supervisors, perpetuates a stereotype, and creates barriers and defensiveness. Some types of inappropriate humor include sarcasm, defensive, hostile, ethnic/racial, or most types of jokes. Generally, jokes are an inappropriate type of humor as they tend to be harmful and not well received. This is because most jokes carry a punch line that is usually a put down, insult or degrading of others. Whereas there are some funny, clean and appropriate jokes, steer away from the jokes aimed at others or those that make individuals or groups the "butt" of the joke. One nice thing about telling a clean joke is there is a good chance that no one has heard it before! It has been speculated that only 3% of the population remembers and tells jokes well. Fortunately, jokes aren't crucial to experiencing humor. It is more important to have fun, than to be funny. Comedy keeps them laughing, humor keeps them smiling!

The 4 NO-NO's of Bad Humor:
- **NO** Sarcasm
- **NO** Ridicule
- **NO** Racial Overtones
- **NO** Put Downs

Appropriate or constructive humor raises self-esteem, reduces tension, fosters laughter with others, breaks down barriers, relaxes people, stimulates new ideas, and creates a positive atmosphere. Appropriate humor is also nurturing humor (positive – laughing with) and brings bonding (victimless). A happy marriage is usually one filled with laughter. So, we encourage you to laugh with your spouse (but don't laugh and point). In general, humor aimed at oneself is well received by others. Learning to laugh at yourself will give you a life-long source of amusement! Appropriate humor should feel good when we experience it. The pleasurable experience is usually accompanied by a smile and a laugh!

Stomper the Clown would soon learn just exactly how
subjective humor can be.

Because everyone's sense of humor is highly individualized, one must be careful when using it, as they run the risk of offending others.

Here are some basic appropriate humor guidelines to help reduce the risk of offending someone.

THE 3 RIGHTS:

1. **RIGHT TIME** – There is a proper time for the use of humor in relationship to an event. At the peak of a crisis, humor will fall flat. Some time may have to elapse before you can use humor. Usually a safe time to use humor is when another person uses humor with you.
2. **RIGHT PLACE** – Regardless of whether or not a person was intended to hear a conversation, it is important to remember that anyone who can hear, see, or experience the humor is a participant.
3. **RIGHT STYLE** – There are many appropriate styles of humor such as:

-   **Exaggeration** - *"My health is so bad, my doctor just advised me not to start reading any long novels!"*
-   **Word Play** - *"Do you know how many drunks there are in the United States? The statistics are staggering!"*
-   **Observational** - A bumper sticker: *"My child was the Inmate of the Month at County Jail!"*
-   **Physical** - Slapstick comedy, silly gestures, or even making a funny face.
-   **Ironies** - How can the United States help other nations negotiate for peace, yet still be the largest exporter of arms in the world?

68

HOW TO BE A HUMOR BEING

"The day most wholly lost is the one
on which one does not laugh!"
Nicolas Chamfort – writer (1740-1794)

QUESTION: It is late at night and a frequent flyer is extremely tired as he boards a red-eye flight for home. As the flyer enters the plane, he notices two empty seats. One seat is next to a gentleman that looks tense, angry, and stressed. The other open seat is next to a gentleman that appears to be happy and smiling. What seat do you think the frequent flyer will take?

ANSWER: The frequent flyer will most likely take the seat next to the angry person. This is because grumpy is less likely to talk to him during the flight!

IDEAS TO CREATE MORE LAUGHTER AND FUN IN YOUR LIFE:

(**WARNING:** The following ideas do come with a side effect; you might laugh until you leak!)

1. Make a list of things that are fun for you and do at least one item daily. You already made a list just like that earlier in the book. Now, start applying it today.
2. See a movie of your choice, especially a comedy, and buy popcorn.
3. Read something funny for enjoyment, like this book.
4. Have a good laugh at yourself. Everyday that you wake up, smile, enjoy, and be happy! Life is so much more fun when its main character, namely you, isn't too self-serious.

5. Put comedy into your commute by listening to humorous books on tape or a funny radio show.

6. Organize a humor library by collecting funny videos, books, cartoons, and jokes. Share these funnies with your family, friends and colleagues. Watch the funny videos whenever you're stressed or blue or for no special reason. (When you're feeling blue, it is highly recommended to start breathing again!)

7. Share your most embarrassing moment or funniest personal story. Submit it to *Readers Digest*. If they publish it, you get paid! The *Readers Digest* submission address is in the back of this book.

8. Use humorous props. (silly glasses, fart machine, picture frame for your desk with pictures of really ugly kids, dart board decision maker, etc.)

9. Get a humor buddy (or four!) Even an email humor buddy will work. Plan play dates with your humor buddy(s).

10. Be open to funny. Let yourself be silly. Most people are just as happy as they make up their mind to be.

A sense of humor is the #1 romantically attractive trait!

HUMORISNOWHERE

Some people will read the above caption as "Humor Is *No* Where," and they would be right!

Some people will read the above caption as "Humor Is *Now* Here" and they would be right also!

As in much of life, what you see is likely to be what you get!

"There are three types of people –
people with a sense of humor and those without!"

OFFICE HUMOR

BENEFITS OF GOOD HUMOR IN THE WORKPLACE:

1. Laughing together creates and reinforces a sense of solidarity.
2. People with a sense of humor are generally more productive than those without.
3. Humor is intellectual play.
4. Humor helps to reframe negative situations and defuse confrontations.
5. Humor can help to prevent burn-out in your professional life.
6. Humor helps improve morale and working relationships.
7. Humor helps bring new perspectives to serious problems or situations.
8. Humor creates communication / connection.

<u>10 ways to put humor into your work</u>

1. **HUMOR SAFARI** – Take pictures of the funny things you see. (Road signs, Bumper stickers, Humans)
   Here are some of the funny things we have seen:
   Bumper Stickers:
   "If you can read this, I can slam on my brakes and sue you"
   "Hang up and drive"
   "Don't like my driving? Then don't watch me"
   "Your ridiculous little opinion has been noted"
   "Officer, will this sticker saying, "I Support Law Enforcement" stop you from giving me a ticket?"
   "Don't tailgate me or I'll flick a booger on your windshield"

Signs:

Wendys, McDonalds, Taco Bell, GAS
Bathroom Closed – for bathroom use stairs below
Ears pierced – half off!

"Life literally abounds in comedy,
if you just look around."
—Mel Brooks

2. **CUBICLE OR LOCKER COMEDY** – Decorate your office or locker with funny signs, posters, or inspirations.
   Signs:
   "Failure to plan on your part does NOT
   constitute an emergency on my part."
   "Computers do more work than people because they never
   have to answer the phone."
   "If you want a quick answer, ask the boss, if you want the
   correct answer, ask the secretary."
   "Please be patient. I only have two speeds. If this one isn't fast
   enough, then I'm sure you won't like the other."
   "Tell me how lucky I am to work here.....I keep forgetting."

3. **HUMORIZE REPORTS** - Humor will add a human touch to enliven your reports and help underscore an important point or message. Consider adding humor, witty words, quotes, funny sayings or observational humor to your writings (i.e. department newsletter, memos, emails, graphs, reports, or minutes.) Also, inject humor into your publications (i.e. catalogs, brochures, sales flyers, policy manuals, etc.)

4. **COMEDY AWARDS** - During a meeting or briefing give out certificates or trophies as comedy awards. This could be a certificate for "driver of the month" to the person who has the most fender benders or a trophy with a diaper on top for a person who just delivered a baby in the line of duty.

5. **HUMANIZE YOUR MEETINGS** – Give a boost to your material as well as to your audience by humanizing your talks.
   Wear weird glasses to the meeting.
   Put your next problem solving meeting in a *"Jeopardy"* format. Open the meeting with a funny or amusing anecdote, self deprecation humor, quirky observations or a story illustrating your point.
   Meetings are a good time to recognize someone from your organization and give them a round of applause. Normally it is only sports stars, singers, actors, etc., that are getting the attention; First responders deserve a good round of applause too.

6. **PLANNED FUN!**
   Celebrations: surprise your staff by having their offices colorfully decorated when they arrive for work on their birthday or anniversary.
   Crazy tie day.
   Plan something crazy on April Fools Day, Ground Hogs Day, National Left-Handers Day.
   Post high school pictures and guess who everyone is.
   Aloha Fridays instead of casual.
   Guess how many jelly beans in the jar contest.

7. **CARTOON CALENDARS** – Ditch your typical boring government calendar. Buy yourself a desk calendar in which you receive a good dose of humor-a-day, or one that supplies inspirational sayings.

8. **WALL OF HUMOR** – In a high traffic area of your office, find a wall where you can post funny articles, cartoons, pictures, quotes, etc. Encourage all staff to add their humor. The humor wall will lighten surroundings, and provide an abundance of entertainment.

9. **NOTEBOOK OF HUMOR** – Start a notebook of cartoons, funny headlines, inspiring quotes, and funny sayings related to your occupation. Encourage others to add their funnies and place the book in an area (latrine) where workers can read and enjoy the fun.

10. **HUMOR TEAM** – Build humor into your department by establishing a humor team whose purpose is to plan and implement a variety of fun activities and events on and off duty throughout the year. If you are in a position of leadership, give your staff permission to have fun and "walk your talk!" Be willing to overcome the fear of foolishness and don't be afraid to look silly by wearing a goofy hat, tie, button, socks, etc. Humor and fun are infectious. There are a growing number of bottom-line successful corporations that have been practicing humor. Southwest Airlines President, Herb Kelleher is well known for his creative shenanigans and modeling humor from the top down. The ice cream company, Ben and Jerry's have established a "Joy Committee," and offer "Joy Grants" to their employees who have an idea that will bring more joy into the workplace.

*This page left intentionally blank
because we just couldn't think of
anything else to write.*

WINDING IT UP

"Knowing something is not enough. You have to do what you know to be effective."
—Jim Rohn, Motivational Speaker

In the preceding chapters we have provided some awareness about stress and its effects. We have also given you some tools to enable you to obtain balance in your life. A lot of ideas in this book are basic ideas and strategies, possibly things you already know. Getting back to basics, however, is always a good thing. By implementing the ideas in this book, it will help you to lessen your anxiety and decrease your sense of isolation in regard to stress related difficulties. Armed with the tools that we have provided herein, you should now be ready to take positive steps to combat your stress. It is said that it takes 21 days to create a habit. We truly hope you take the time to make the "Triad of Balance" a habit in your life. By doing so you will learn to lighten up, stress less, and take life less seriously. To make this happen, though, you must first have the desire. If you really want to do something, you'll find a way; if you don't, you'll find an excuse. It is said, "A journey of a thousand miles starts with one step." An argument can be made, though, that the journey actually started with the desire to go on the "journey." To reduce the stress in your life, you must first have the desire to do just that. Remember, balance is only temporary, and in life, the unexpected happens. So, be ready!

STORY

For thirty years a man sat on a street corner on top of a wooden box begging for money. One day a stranger walked by him. As he did, the beggar asked him, "Can you spare some change?" The stranger answered, "I have nothing to give, but what is that you're sitting on?" The beggar answered, "An old box." The stranger then asked, "What's in it?" The beggar replied, "I don't know." Now curious about the contents of the wooden box', the two men pried open the lid of the box and found it filled with gold!

We, the authors of this book, are the stranger who has nothing to give you and is telling you to look inside your box. Not inside a figurative box, but inside yourself. But then you think, "I am not a beggar." Those who have not found true balance, however, are beggars, even if they have great material wealth. It may be possible that you are still looking for scraps of pleasure or fulfillment, for validation, security, or love. You don't have far to look. Open the box that you have been sitting on for all those years and you'll find a treasure—a balanced life.

BUL – YAW!

Balance Ur Life – You'll Always Win

"Everything will be fine in the end. If it's not fine, it's not the end."

FIRST RESPONDER'S COMICAL ANECDOTES FOR STRESS

The following pages contain over one-hundred-and-fifty first responder's contributions: stories, poems, art work, and true-to-life anecdotes. Some are comical, others are heart touching, while some are just plain unbelievable. They are, however, all true accounts from the brave men and women we call first responders. The contributions come from firefighters, EMS personnel, and police officers from all fifty United States, Washington D.C, and five foreign countries. In addition to the stories from first responders, we have also collected some from the people that support first responders—the mechanics, electricians, and other support staff that keep the wheels of justice and safety rolling. We have also added some fun facts and educational information for additional reading while you're on the road to obtaining a balanced life. So, sit back, find a nice quiet place, and get ready to enjoy the, "First Responders Handbook of Humor" collection of stories which we have complied for your reading pleasure.

FIRE

MISSING IN ACTION—ALMOST

Over the years many changes have occurred in the fire service, mostly because of safety concerns. One of these changes is that the Los Angeles City Fire Department has discontinued the practice of traveling to an incident on the back of the fire engine. The following story, however, occurred long ago, when half the fun was surfing the tailboard to the fire. It was just another typical day at the fire station. There were personnel scattered about, some doing work in the front office, while one fireman enjoyed private time in the backyard with a loved one. Suddenly, the dispatch bell rang, and the words, "structure fire," blared across the PA system. Everyone immediately dropped what they were doing and ran for the fire engine—everyone, that is, except Fireman "A," who, at the time, was actively busy in the backyard and didn't hear the alarm sound. With the engineer thinking everyone was present, he started the engine and prepared to leave. Not wanting to leave his partner behind, Fireman "B" jumped off the tailboard in search of his missing friend. Unfortunately, he didn't notify the rest of his crew that he was leaving. Quickly running to the backyard, Fireman "B" found his partner, and the two returned just in time to see the engine pull out of the station without them. The two immediately decided to chase after the engine on foot; however, unable to catch them, they quickly gave up. All of a sudden, a rescue ambulance pulled up next to them. The firemen hastily explained the situation, and the race was on. With brake-neck speed, the ambulance chased down the engine, luckily catching up to it just as it pulled up to the fire. Before anyone was the wiser, the two firemen ran to the back of the engine and climbed on the tailboard just as the captain turned around and shouted the order to hook up to the hydrant. To this day, only the firemen, the ambulance personnel, and now you, know the truth. They say God watches over drunks and firefighters. I know of at least two firefighters that would have to agree with that!
Engineer Kirk

Bottoms Up

Even the best of plans sometimes go wrong. Fortunately, with training and experience, first responders make the best out of a bad situation and sometimes have fun doing it. Responding to a man down call, Lieutenant Mike Gurr, from a Florida fire company, and his crew discovered an elderly man down on a wooden boat dock. Being forewarned of the dock's deteriorating condition, Lt. Gurr decided to let the lighter members of his crew assess the man while his larger frame body assisted on the concrete seawall next door. Unbeknownst to him and his crew, the dock was in worse shape than first thought, and while attempting to put the older man on a backboard, the wooden dock gave way, dropping all involved eight feet down into the deep water canal below. Fear for his crew quickly set in as Lt. Gurr raced back to the truck for a rope. Upon his return, though, fear turned to laughter as he saw the patient doing his best impression of an ostrich—his butt sticking straight up in the air, and his face buried in the murky mud below. If that wasn't enough, Lt. Gurr next spotted the man's hairpiece floating by, heading out to sea. Luckily, all involved were not seriously hurt. It just goes to show you, all's well that *ENDS* well.

Mike Gurr, Lieutenant, Florida

MOVE TO THE RIGHT FOR SIRENS AND LIGHTS!

CASPER THE FRIENDSHIP GHOST

Every state highway system has its problems with potholes—the state of Alabama being no exception. While traveling down Highway 280 towards a reported vehicle fire, a pumper truck staffed by two fire-fighters, an assistant chief, and a lead firefighter of the Friendship Fire Department accidentally hit one of these menaces of the road. Fortunately, being a newer truck, the vehicle was equipped with air-cushioned seats which floated up as designed to soften the ride. Unfortunately, as the seat came downward with gravity, it struck a fire extinguisher that had come loose from its bracket and lodged itself under the driver's seat. The shearing down force of the seat caused it to break the top of the extinguisher off, spewing its entire chemical contents into the cab and onto its occupants. As the blinding white cloud filled the inside of the truck, the firefighters were forced to bring the pumper to a screeching stop, bailing out, luckily unharmed, but looking more like Casper the Ghost than Friendship Firefighters.

Angelia Richards, Deputy Chief. Friendship Firefighters Association, Alabama

JUST THE FACTS

At the Battle of Mobile Bay located in Alabama, Admiral David Farragut issued his famous command, "Damn the torpedoes, full speed ahead." The event occurred on August 5, 1864.

DEVOTION

Last night, again, I wasn't home when I had said I'd be.
I realize you seldom know what might be keeping me.

I had a meeting at the church, which was to end at eight,
But when the clock struck more than ten, you knew I'd be home late.

Just when the meeting was to close, my pager let me know
That someone really needed help and I was there to go.

I was returning from that call and nearly home to you,
The pager tripped a second time and so I went there, too.

Now, these two calls were medical and not as dangerous
As fires, auto accidents, or scenes more perilous.

You have expressed concern for me regardless of the call.
Emergencies all carry risk, albeit, some are small.

You never have complained of times when I have made you wait,
Or rushed from meals or gathering or quit an evening date.

I know you sacrifice the most 'cause you can't see or hear
Expressions of deep gratitude, when I help ease their fear.

Chief Darryl Claassen, Whitewater River Fire District, Kansas

MUTUAL AID

Take one rookie cop, add in a couple of his fellow police officers, and just for fun, top it off with a few firefighters, and you now have the recipe for a great practical joke. At least a group of police officers and firefighters in Bartlett, Illinois, think so. With the group of first responders having such a good working relationship, one veteran police officer called the local fire station informing the crew to get ready to pull a fast one on a rookie cop. By chance, an hour or so before this all began; an unlucky deer was accidentally struck and killed by an auto nearby. The impact from the collision caused the deer to bite off a 2-3 inch piece of its tongue. Seeing a devilish opportunity present itself, one of the police officers on scene of the accident picked up a piece of tongue and brought it back with him to the station. A short time later, he ran into the next shifts roll call and told a rookie cop that the tongue he was carrying belonged to an assault victim, and that the paramedics at the local fire station were waiting for it so that they could emergency transport it to the hospital for re-implantation. Setting the scene for the rookie, the firefighters pulled the ambulance out onto the driveway, turned on the red lights, and waited for the rookie cop to arrive. A few minutes later he arrived in a non-emergent mode, which a firefighter quickly made an issue of, due to the "possibility that the tongue could have died going so long without proper care." Taking the deer tongue from the rookie cop, the firefighters hastily placed it on a cot, inserted an IV in it, and then applied the leads from the cardiac monitor, which to no surprise to the firefighters, showed a flat line on the monitor's display. Suddenly, one of the firefighter/paramedics blew up in an emotional outburst, picking up the tongue and throwing it into a garbage can. He then quickly turned to the rookie officer and blamed him for the tongue's death due to him taking his sweet time delivering it. The look on the cop's face was one of total dismay.

After several humble apologies from the distraught officer, all of the first responders present started laughing and soon let him in on the practical joke. Needless to say, first responders from both departments are now looking over their shoulders for the payback.

David Misner, Lieutenant. Bartlett Fire Protection District. Illinois

JUST THE FACTS

The name "Illinois" came from the Algonquin word *Inini*, meaning "the men" and "accomplished."

DUDE, WHERE'S YOUR TRUCK?

First responders know that in order to be successful in their job, they must employ creativity, ingenuity, and an attitude to help, no matter what obstacles might get in their way. Bill Davis, a firefighter in Madison Township-Franklin County, Ohio, shares a story in which he had to utilize his creative prowess. Like many of the other volunteer firefighters in the department, Davis lives in a nearby residential area, relatively close to the station. Typically, the firefighters keep their gear in their personal vehicles and respond directly to the scene of an emergency. The firefighters living closest to the station have the responsibility to report to the station first, pick up the fire trucks, and then respond to the scene. Because of this procedure, the response time for some of the firefighters is expedited, while others are scattered. Many times the firefighters responding by car will arrive on scene of the emergency, quickly dress in their gear, and be ready to go well before the fire trucks arrive. On one such occasion, Davis and a few other firefighters arrived at a residential fire prior to the trucks. Once there, they quickly discovered a smoldering mattress fire in the house. Dragging the mattress outside, they used a garden hose to extinguish the fire. Upon seeing this, one of the neighbors questioned, *"Don't they use fire trucks anymore?"*

Bill Davis, Firefighter. Madison Township-Franklin County, Ohio

FOLLOWING COMMANDS

Being shorthanded at the scene of an emergency is nothing new to Lieutenant Doug Myers of the Niles Township Fire Department. Unfortunately, being a smaller department, he is often forced to respond with only one full-time firefighter on the engine and has to depend on on-call personnel to meet them at the scene of an emergency. Responding to a house fire with only two firefighters, one of which was a probationary firefighter that was still in school and could not enter the house due to regulations, Lt. Myers made the best of the situation as he waited for the remaining on-call personnel to arrive. He accomplished this by pulling off a 200 foot section of pre-connected hose and handed it, along with the attached nozzle, to the "probie." He then pointed down the driveway towards the road. *"Take this, go that way,"* was his command to the rookie firefighter, and that is exactly what he did. Unfortunately, instead of stretching out the hose to it's 100 foot midpoint, and then returning with the nozzle end, the rookie went the whole 200 feet, pulling the line taut to the end of the driveway where he was met by other incoming fire companies. This caused Lt. Myers to ask one of the arriving firefighters to retrieve the nozzle so they could attack the fire. Later the "probie" apologized for his actions, to which Lt. Myers replied, *"You did exactly as you were told, and you're good to go in my book."*

Doug Myers, Lieutenant. Niles Township Fire Department. Michigan

LESSONS LEARNED

The Captain of Sedgwick County Fire District #1 looked at his fire-fighter driver with bloodshot eyes as they pulled away from a structure fire. It had been a long night, battling not just the fire, but also a stiff Kansas wind and snow on a bone chilling, ten degree January morning. Thankfully, their engine company was the first to be released from the stubborn blaze, making themselves available and heading back to the station to get some dry clothes and a hot cup of coffee. As they made their way, water dripped from their upper lips, the result of the rig's heater melting the frozen ice in their moustaches. Suddenly, the pumper's motor became eerily silent, the engine eventually coasting to a complete stop. The driver tried everything he could to restart the engine, but to no avail. With the chill of the early morning creeping into the cab, the captain called the duty mechanic and informed him what had occurred. The mechanic theorized that the problem was probably a frozen fuel filter. Figuring the mechanic would have to access an engine panel to change the filter out, the two firefighters went to work on removing it. Unfortunately, they quickly found the panel frozen shut. Now, it is important to note here that the word "immovable" does not exist in a firefighter's vocabulary. Grabbing the universal unlocking tool, (i.e. a rubber mallet) the captain began gingerly banging away at the ice around the panel, being extra careful not to chip any of the paint on the new fire engine. Another important thing to note here is that patience is not a virtue of many firefighters. The firefighter stood nearby, watching in agony at his commander's slow progress on the panel. Offering to take a shot at removing the panel, the firefighter took the enormous, black mallet from the captain who reluctantly handed it over. As the fire-fighter mentally prepared himself to wail away at the stubborn panel, the captain stepped forward to offer one last bit of advice; this would be a mistake. As the firefighter took a huge swing at the ice-incrusted metal panel, he felt something odd occur during his back swing.

Completing the stroke and shattering the ice on the panel into small pieces, the firefighter looked back to find his captain sitting on the frozen ground, blinking his eyes profusely, and unable to focus. The firefighter next observed a small trickle of blood running down the captain's nose as he heard the man exclaim in not so nice of a tone, "I think you broke my nose, I think you broke my @#$& nose!" Seeing this, the firefighter realized he had clobbered his captain silly on his back swing. Noting no serious harm had come to the man, the firefighter began to chuckle slightly. He then quickly turned away, and covered his mouth to muffle the more intense laughter that was welling up inside him. Unable to contain himself any longer, the firefighter sank to his knees, then like a volcano, unleashed his trapped emotions in an explosion of laughter. Huge tears froze to the firefighter's face as he tried to contain himself. The captain was less moved. He repeatedly shouted, "You broke my nose! I think you broke my nose." The captain then in a show of horseplay, attempted to silence his tormentor's laughter by playfully punching and kicking him. The punches, though, only seemed to bring out the masochism in the firefighter; for the more the captain struck him, the harder the firefighter laughed. That day the men learned two valuable lessons. 1) Give a directive and get the hell out of the way! 2) Apologies seem much more sincere if you are not rolling on the ground, laughing hysterically.

Robert Conger, Captain. Sedgwick County Fire District #1. Wichita, Kansas

After learning of the disaster in New York on 9/11, Susan D. Wiseman expressing her thoughts and emotions, as the tragedy *unfolded began* writing this song, known as... ***God Will Prevail -"The Victim's Anthem"***

"DEDICATED TO GOD...&...NEVER ENDING FREEDOM"

GOD WILL PREVAIL –
"THE VICTIMS' ANTHEM"

When the dust has settled and the rubble's cleared,
And, the hole that's left was all we feared;
When the strength of man has finally failed...
God, Will Prevail!

When the last poor soul's been laid to rest,
In this sea of tears and endless lists;
That, is when you'll see her rise above...
God, Will Prevail!

For, Freedom... Still Rings,
Through This Land!

America, Forever... Will Stand,
In God's Hands!

And, When The Strength Of Man
Finally... Fails,
God, Will Prevail!

Though all the walls have crumbled and fall down,
As our dreams lie scattered on this ground;

You will see her rise from bended knees...
God, Will Prevail... Again!

For, Freedom... Still Rings,
Through This Land!

America, Forever... Shall Stand,
In God's Hands!

As We Soar, Through the Skies
You Will See,

That, America's... Still Brave
She'll Still Fight
For... Liberty!

But, if America...
Should ever, fail...

God's Will... Prevail!

Words and Music
©Copyright September 2001 by Susan D. Wiseman,

Fayetteville, Georgia

www.susandwiseman.com -   *Susan D. Wiseman... a housewife
with a music ministry called "Christ-Centered Pieces"- Given Gifts.
Susan records out of passion and conviction and dedicates much of
her work to America's firefighters, policemen, rescue workers, military
and the world.*   **ALL....Downloads ...are ...FREE!**

FIREFIGHTER SAVES CAT IN TREE

Everyone loves firefighters. The classic tale of the "Firefighter Saves Cat in Tree," only adds to the adulations. After twelve years in the fire service, though, Firefighter Kent Mallette of Broken Bow, Nebraska, had never experienced such a rescue. All that changed one day as he was diligently working at his new management job when a police officer called the station and requested a firefighter to come to his location with a ladder. Mallette immediately drove the fire truck to the reported address and was met by the officer standing with a small girl about six-years old and her mother. When Mallette asked what was wrong, the little girl started crying as she pointed to her cat fifteen feet up in the tree. Seizing the opportunity to be a hero to this little girl, Mallette retrieved a ladder from his truck and started his assent into the tree. When he got close to the cat, he sensed it was extremely frightened by the death grip it had on a branch. Grabbing for it, the once cute, loveable pet instantly transformed into the "Spawn of Satan," complete with razor sharp claws. The cat's fur rose up and it quickly struck out at the rescuer. Unfortunately, the bunker gear gloves Mallette wore were no match for the cat's sharp claws that tore into the firefighter's hand. After the attack, the cat then ran higher up in the tree. By this time, Mallette was thinking to himself that the police officer's gun would be a good solution for the cat. Looking down at the little girl, Mallette shook off the pain in his shredded hand, refocusing himself on rescuing the cat. With renewed enthusiasm, he continued the climb higher, again nearing the cat. This time, Mallette took some time to let the cat calm down enough for him to pet it. He was then able to scoop up the cat and cradle it under his arm for the decent down the ladder. On the way down, though, the kitty decided he didn't like being carried under a firefighter's arm; so it attacked again, biting and clawing its way to freedom. The price of freedom was high that day. Not only did it cost the cat a nice long drop to the ground, about twelve feet, but it also caused the heroic rescuer his pride, and almost his life as he fell backwards off the ladder, landing awkwardly in a heap of broken branches and leaves. Dusting off the mess, Mallette looked over and saw the little girl holding her now docile kitty. After securing the cat in the house, the little girl gave her hero firefighter a big hug, making the rescue all worth it.

Kent Mallette, Fire Chief. Broken Bow, Nebraska.

JUST THE FACTS

The 911 system of emergency communications, now used nationwide, was developed and first used in Lincoln, Nebraska.

SNAKE CHARMER

Snakes can be a dangerous thing, especially if they belong to your five-year-old son. Called out on a reported snake call, Firefighter/Paramedic John Hicks of the Los Angeles City Fire Department and his engine company, arrived at a residence to find a middle aged woman, along with her two young children standing on the driveway. The woman, who was visibly upset, was frantically pointing to her house. Calming her down, Hicks obtained the details about a large snake occupying her living room. Peering through the woman's front window, Hicks observed the snake, extended upright in a striking position, reminding him of a cobra in a bad foreign movie. Prepared for battle with their proper protective gear, Hicks and his partner next entered the residence to find the snake in the same exact position, standing its ground against all who would approach. As the woman safely watched from outside the window, Hicks approach the snake with due caution. Seeing his chance, he darted forward, grabbing the vicious creature with his bare hands. After a short, hazardous struggle, Hicks subdued the reptile, squeezing the last remnants of its life from its plastic body. Yes, you read it correctly—plastic. It turns out that the dangerous snake was really a toy that belonged to one of the woman's children. To say the least, the woman was not charmed by Hicks' academy award winning performance, giving him a cold, plastic stare of her own as he left the scene.

John B. Hicks, Firefighter/Paramedic. Los Angles City Fire Department, California

ON THIN ICE

In any language a child in danger translates into quick action by first responders. Early one Christmas season, first responders from the Hermsdorf Volunteer Fire Department received an alert that a child had broken through the ice while playing a game. Leading the group into action was Marcel Hartman, the Chief of the Department. With the local fire department already in the water with boats, Chief Hartman ordered his crew to build up lampposts (floodlights) to illuminate the area since it was getting dark. As the firemen continued the search, a large crowd started to form. Chief Hartman continued to supervise his team when a young boy, about 7 years of age, came up to him and asked him why there were so many fire department vehicles in the area. The chief replied that they were looking for a child who was playing in the area and had disappeared. They had found a hole in the ice and thought he might have fallen in. Hearing this, the boy replied, "I was playing here and fell in a hole, but I just got my feet wet. I got cold, so I went home." Quickly realizing the young boy standing next to him was the individual they had been searching for, the relieved chief took the boy over to his comrades, cheerfully exclaiming that he was the one they were looking for. After the long three-hour search, laughter warmed their hearts and the firemen were glad to return the boy to his parents, giving them the best Christmas gift they would ever receive.

Marcel Hartman, Chief. Hermsdorf Volunteer Fire Department. Hermsdorf, Germany

PIZZA, PIZZA

Where has all the common sense gone? That's the question Battalion Chief Stephen Rich of the Canton, Ohio Fire Department asked himself after one particular call. Responding to a report of a structure fire, the chief and his crew arrived on scene of an older two-story home with the front porch on fire. After making a quick knock down of the blaze, the firefighters found people still inside the structure. With the fire being of suspicious nature, arson investigators were called out to investigate. During the course of the investigation, it was learned that the occupants of the house had a pizza delivered just prior to the fire being called in. Quickly determining who delivered the pizza, the delivery man was summoned back to the scene. When the delivery man arrived, the arson investigator asked him if he had seen anything suspicious while delivering the pizza. The delivery man stated he did see a fire on the front porch. Scratching his head, the investigator then asked the man if he saw the fire, why didn't he alert anyone to the danger. The delivery man replied, "As I approached the porch, I saw a sign on the front door that read 'Use the Side Door.' I thought they put that sign on the door because the porch was on fire." Hopefully the delivery man is not putting himself through medical school by delivering pizzas.

Stephen J. Rich, Division Chief. Canton Ohio Fire Department. Ohio

JUST THE FACTS

The first ambulance service was established in Cincinnati in 1865.

Captain David Griffith of the Durham Fire Department, North Carolina has had a long and successful career as a fire officer. Throughout his career he has documented the funny and unusual on-duty events he has encountered by means of skillfully illustrating cartoons. The following cartoon is an example of his work.

Yes, there are reports of snakes in the house. We have specialists on the scene dealing with that now.

A structure fire dispatch several blocks away from Station 2 summoned a two alarm response. The first in company made an attack in one side of the duplex apartment, and other crews fought fire extension into the adjoining apartment. As the smoke began to clear, someone noticed that the floor was full of broken terrarium containers and snakes! It seems that the resident was breeding poisonous snakes for their venom to produce and sell serum for snake bites. The heat and smoke conditions luckily rendered the creatures into a docile state, and no one was bitten. We always wondered if all of the snakes were recovered.

THE BUZZ AROUND TOWN

Years back while working on a weekend shift, Firefighter/Paramedic Doug Rice of the Unified Fire Authority of Greater Salt Lake, Utah, was finishing up lunch. All of a sudden the station and surrounding area had a momentary power outage. The captain, a gruff old-timer who was sitting with him quipped, "Well, there's our next call. Someone must have hit a power pole." Sure enough, about 15 minutes after the outage, Rice and his fire company received a call for a reported house fire. A full assignment of men and equipment was sent to the address. Arriving on scene, the first responders were met at the driveway by the homeowners of a two-story house with the garage door and all the windows open. The man of the house explained that he had just returned home from a round of golf when his wife told him that they had a power outage. She then told him that following the power failure, a new 32-inch television that they had in their bedroom started smoking and buzzing. After gathering the necessary information, a three-man team headed inside while the rest of the firefighters, along with the homeowners, waited outside. Entering the master bedroom, the team of firefighters found the 32-inch TV sitting on a small nightstand. It wasn't smoking at the time; however, there was still a loud buzzing noise coming from it. Finding that it had already been unplugged, the captain and the two firefighters were puzzled, wondering what could be causing the noise. The captain then suggested they take a look behind the set. Being as cautious as possible just in case the TV's coil was still energized with electricity, the firefighters tilted the set forward to view the back. As the T.V was tilted, the nightstand began to rock forward, causing one of its drawers to slide open. There, nestled in a cushion of lace and silk lingerie, was the cause of the buzzing—a vibrator! When the team of firefighters explained to the homeowners what had caused the buzzing, the wife turned twenty shades of red and ran inside the house. Her husband, though, took it another way, almost busting a gut with laughter. If things weren't already bad enough for the wife, the husband then turned to his neighbors and explained that the trouble was not so much in his new television set, but in his wife's toy chest instead! Hope the guy was comfortable on the couch that night!

Doug Rice, Captain. Unified Fire Authority of Greater Salt Lake. Utah.

JUST THE FACTS

The largest public employer in Utah is the Utah State Government.

REED KINDLE

Beginning a career in firefighting in 1954, Grandpa Budd Pitcher has paved the way for generations of firefighters, having one son and four grandchildren in the fire service. To this day, Grandpa Pitcher himself is still semi-active as a volunteer firefighter with the Smithfield Fire Department in Utah. One of his grandchildren, Robert Pitcher, a firefighter for the same department tells us of one of his favorite stories about his Grandfather. Back some years ago, Firefighter Budd Pitcher had responded to a laundry mat fire, spending most of that summer day extinguishing and overhauling it. With the blaze finally out, the senior firefighter retired for the night, taking a well-deserved slumber in his apartment which was located right above the town's fire station. Back then, the firefighters would receive their alarms by way of the town air-raid siren. With Grandpa Budd fast asleep, and his faithful wife lying by his side, an alarm sounded at midnight. Sitting on Budd's nightstand was a scanner, which monitored the town's emergency radio transmissions. The half-asleep firefighter awoke to the sound of the air-raid siren. Sitting up in bed, he then listened as the scanner broadcast the alarm, "Smithfield firemen. Please respond to a rekindle at the laundry mat." Questioning the dispatch, the groggy firefighter woke up his wife, asking her, "Who in God's name is Reed Kindle?" To this day, this humorous story is still shared at family gatherings, and hopefully for further generations to come.

Robert Pitcher, Firefighter. Smithfield Fire Department. North Smithfield, Utah

THE DOMINO EFFECT

If some people didn't have bad luck, they wouldn't have any luck at all. At least that's the opinion of Captain Kenneth Moore of the Eastwood Volunteer Fire Department. Called out to a rural part of West Virginia, for a reported brush fire, Moore and a team of firefighters discovered a pile of trash, two storage buildings, and one tree that were all on fire. After using approximately 2,500 gallons of water to completely extinguish the flames, Moore approached the landowner to investigate the cause of the blaze. The man explained that he was burning a pile of trash close to one of his storage buildings. The man went on to further explain that because he had enough room in a newer and larger building that was just built six feet from an older and smaller one, he let the trash fire extend onto the older structure to rid himself of it. Armed with only a garden hose, he watched anxiously as the trash fire extended onto the older building as planned, and then unexpectedly onto the larger one. Before he knew it, the fire again jumped in length, spreading uncontrollably to a tree that was within 200 feet. To add insult to injury, the owner next had to endure a nice long talk with an officer from the Department of Natural Resources, who issued the landowner a number of citations. Nothing like job security!

Kenneth Moore, Captain. Eastwood Volunteer Fire Department. West Virginia

JUST THE FACTS

The first federal prison exclusively for women in the United States was opened in 1926 in West Virginia.

CAPTAIN LOTTO FEVER

Everyone dreams of playing the lotto and striking it rich. Even first responders are not immune from this fantasy. One such fire captain was especially mesmerized with this idea. Each week he would buy a lotto ticket in hopes of retiring early. Like clockwork, he would turn on the television at the appropriate time to see the six little ping-pong shaped balls drop onto the rail, revealing the winning numbers. He would win five dollars here, a dollar there. He once even won fifty dollars. Nevertheless, the big one always seemed to elude him. His luck, though, was about to change; at least he would be made to believe so. For unbeknownst to him, his crew had taped the lottery show a few weeks before. They then went out and bought a ticket containing those exact winning numbers from that show. When they were next asked to buy him a ticket while they were doing their daily shopping for mess, they just simply gave him that ticket. The plot was now set. Saturday night soon rolled around with the captain being none the wiser. With the television and VCR on, the crew started the tape just as he walked into the room. The wide-eyed pigeon, believing he was watching a live broadcast, stared in amazement as one after another winning number somehow magically appeared on his ticket. Like a young schoolboy getting out of class for the day, the man jumped up out of his seat as the last number was read. Yells and cheers emanated from his mouth as he danced around the station, now thinking he was a millionaire. The crew joined in his celebration, playing the gag for all that it was worth. However, even the best laid plans sometimes go bad, and this particular one was about to get ugly. Unfortunately, for the unsuspecting crew, this individual did not get along with his superior, the chief. With all common sense out the door, and thinking this was his last day of work anyway, he proceeded to call his boss and tell him what he really thought of him. The crew sat there with their mouths wide open and hearts pounding as their commander continued to enlighten his superior on his

true feelings for him. Knowing the joke had now gone past the point of fun, the crew immediately stopped him mid-conversation and confessed their trickery. To say the least, he was not amused. The scorned captain quickly apologized to his chief, playing it off as a misunderstanding. The chief, being a good sport, dismissed it as such and went about his business. The captain's crew, however, would not get off so easy. Although particulars are not well known, the rumor is that midnight drills are still part of their daily routine.

Name withheld per request. Los Angeles, California

How is it that one careless match
can start a forest fire,
but it takes a whole box
to start a camp fire?

ALARMING BEHAVIOR

Malfunctioning fire detection systems are a common call for fire departments across the country. While most are simply a nuisance, resulting in a false alarm and supplying a dose of aggravation for all concerned, once in a while they do prove entertaining. Responding to such a call to investigate a smoke detector sounding in a new home located on base, Captain Frank Johnson of the Fort Bragg Fire Department quickly determined there was in fact no emergency. He did, however, discover a malfunctioning fire system that had been wired altogether causing all the smoke detectors in the house to sound in unison. Unable to locate the exact problem, Captain Johnson ordered his crew to remove all the detectors from the walls in an attempt to silence the problem. A short time passed, and Johnson continued to hear one detector sounding, and it also seemed to be changing locations. Noticing the sound nearing, Johnson turned to find one of his men standing behind him. The firefighter began explaining to the captain that all the detectors were off the walls; however, he was unable to locate the one still causing the ear-piercing sound. Aware that smoke detectors have a battery back up, Captain Johnson simply looked at the firefighter and replied, "You might want to check the one in your hand!"

Frank Johnson, Captain. Fire Station 3. Directorate of Emergency Services. Fort Bragg, North Carolina

BEARLY SAVED

The main reason firefighters train so hard is to save lives. One fall day, Firefighter David Szymanski got his chance to put his training to good use! He and the rest of the volunteer fire crew responded to a structure fire alarm. On scene the firefighter witnessed a fire showing from one room. Standing outside the structure stood a young mother covered in blood, frantically breaking windows in an attempt to rescue her three young children. A fire attack team quickly entered the house with a charged line to extinguish the fire as the chief directed Szymanski to take a second line in and locate the children. Unfortunately, the cinder block construction kept the heat and smoke of the fire contained to the building, causing extreme heat and poor visibility for Szymanski as he crawled down the dark hallway. Entering the first room, Szymanski started his search, feeling around the room with his gloved hands. Searching near a child's desk he discovered a small leg, the body of which was covered by a clump of clothes. With his heart swelling up into his throat, Szymanski quickly shouted, "Found one," as he simultaneously scooped up the clothes and the lifeless body and made his way outside. Preparing to do CPR, Szymanski removed the clothes that were piled on top of the body, revealing not a human, but a large stuffed teddy bear instead! Luckily, it was later discovered that the three young children were not home at the time of the fire but were found safe in town.

David Szymanski, Public Information Officer. Bellevue Volunteer Fire and Rescue. Nebraska

"Support Search and Rescue-Get Lost!"

105

DON'T SWEAT THE SMALL STUFF

"Don't sweat the small stuff. That sweat will be needed later when the bells ring." A simply philosophy of Firefighter Mathew J. Byers, yet one that is sadly lost in today's world. Still the same, Byers, a TSgt. with the fire protection unit of the 193rd SOW PA Air National Guard, does his best to keep those words in his mind when trouble arises. Learning this mindset early in his career, he often passes along to his troops the story that was initially responsible for this thinking. Luckily, he now passes it along to us. While working as a firefighter with the Millerstown Volunteer Fire Department located in Greenwood TWP, Perry County, Pennsylvania, Byers and the rest of the crew were faced with the mother of all rain storms which caused the worst flooding in years to hit the area. With local rivers and creeks rising to dangerous levels, the nearby roads became unusable. This caused people along the banks of the rivers to become trapped. With the treacherous rushing water as much as four feet above the roads, Byers and his crew, working together as a three-man team, used a tractor to cross the swift moving water to rescue some of the trapped people. Arriving at a dwelling, the men carefully waded up to the steps of a trailer, and the fire chief went inside. There he found the water quickly rising and knew they had to evacuate the people right away. Standing outside, Byers stood anxiously waiting to help. He would not wait too long. Stepping back outside, the chief handed Byers a lump of towels, telling him to be extra careful with them because there was an infant wrapped inside. Different emotions started to flood the young firefighter's senses: nervousness, fear, and even a bit of anger, thinking he would have to listen to the young infant cry all the way back to safety. Keeping the baby under wraps, Byers quickly made his way back to the tractor, doing his best not to fall into the swelling waters. Surprisingly, he didn't hear as much as a peep from the young infant. Settling into the cab of the tractor, Byers began to unwrap the baby from the towels, waiting for the scared baby to start crying as soon as he saw his rescuer's muddied face for the first time. Instead of a cry, however, Byers was greeted with a warm smile and a cheerful laugh in the midst of all the destruction. To this day, TSgt. Byers remembers the infant's laugh, proving to him that stress it not the same for everyone; it's just how one perceives it.

TSgt. Mathew J. Byers. Fire Protection, 193 SOW PA Air National Guard. Middletown, Pennsylvania

TORNADO WATCH

In the fire service, it is always tough being the new guy. This is especially true when you're a probationary firefighter for the United States Air Force. Back in 2001, Mathew J. Byers, a SSgt with the 436th Civil Engineering Squadron/436 Air Lift Wing at Dover Air Force Base, Delaware, said they would occasionally put the new guy on "Tornado Watch." Placing a chair out near the base flight line, they would have the new firefighter/airman shine a flashlight towards the control tower every ten minutes, signaling to the air traffic controller inside that all was clear. The veteran pranksters would then call the base police, who were in on the joke, and have them investigate the unsuspecting individual on the flight line. Because the rookie firefighter didn't have the proper identification to be on a secure flight line yet, the base police would quickly arrest "Airman Newbie." Shortly there after, the fire crew would come and retrieve the rookie, having a good laugh with all involved, and welcoming the new guy to the team.

Dover AFB, Delaware

FIRE TRUCKS AND HANDCUFFS

"Stay cool, man! They just probably want to tell us we have a broken tail light or something."

Parting with personal belongings is sometimes hard to do, and cars are no exception. For a firefighter with the Durham, North Carolina Fire Department, the decision to part with his 1989 Buick was made much easier when he eyed a new vehicle he wanted to purchase. The firefighter immediately placed his used vehicle on a car lot in Creedmore, NC, to be sold. Since he would no longer be driving the car, he promptly cancelled the insurance. Before the car was sold, though, it was stolen off the lot. Once the theft was reported to the disappointed firefighter, he spread the word throughout the department to be on alert for the missing Buick. Shortly thereafter, Durham Fire Captain Chuck Milligan was inside the office of the PIO (Public Information Officer) when he heard a radio call from Ladder 1 to the communicator, reporting they were following a stolen car and their location. Captain Milligan continued to monitor the radio as Ladder 1 broadcast their direction of travel, turn by turn. As the pursuit progressed, Captain Milligan started getting concerned for the safety of the fire crew thinking the thieves could be armed, and expecting at anytime to hear a call of "shots fired." The ladder company continued its pursuit as the stolen car made one final turn into a cul-de-sac, where the ladder truck blocked any chance for escape. The police, who were notified of the situation, immediately responded and made the arrest of the thieves. Luckily, the stolen car was returned undamaged to the grateful owner.

Chuck Milligan, Captain (Ret.) Durham Fire Department, North Carolina. Cartoon illustrated by David Griffith, Captain. Durham Fire Department, North Carolina.

"Yesterday I parked my car in a tow-away zone...When I came back, the entire area was missing!"—Steve Wright

ESCARGOT

Whether you're in the fire service or police department or even the Air Force, at some time or another in your career, you will work with someone that is less than motivated to do their job. In the world of first responders, we call these people "slugs." Scott Rath, currently a Federal Fire Captain stationed at Fort Sam Houston, Texas, began his fire-fighting career with a tour of duty at Torrejon Air Base, Spain. This was the place where he met his first slug, an unmotivated airman basic that was new to the station. As most would in his position, Rath took the junior airman under his wing and showed him the ropes. Try as he may, though, he just couldn't get the airman to conform to the simplest of tasks. Besides having poor hygiene, the airman also had a very abusive personality. One night while off duty, the slug had an altercation with one of their host nation's females. Apparently, he wanted a date and she didn't. What truly transpired after that is not clear, but the next day the slug came to work with a broken nose. That night, at approximately 2: 00 a.m., an alarm came into the station. Quickly waking up as he always did, Rath dashed to his stall, donned his protective gear, and then strapped himself to the back of the truck. A short time passed and Rath hadn't pushed the button on the back to give the driver the okay to take off. As usual, he was waiting for the slug to slither to the truck. With the crew chief yelling "let's go," the less-than-fine young fire-fighter finally made it to the truck, strapped himself in, and said he was ready. Rath looked over at the man as he stood there, helmet on, his nose broken, with bloody mucus running into his matted mustache. With his eyes barely open, the airman appeared half asleep. Giving him a good look up and down, Rath couldn't believe his eyes. As the clock was ticking, Rath stepped off the tailboard, walked around to his crew chief, and told him he needed to see this. The crew chief jumped off the truck, walked around to the back and saw the Air Force's finest, standing there perplexed, asking what was wrong. The crew chief began to laugh uncontrollably. Not only had the slug forgotten to don his bunker pants and boots, he had also forgotten to don anything else, standing there nude. Needless to say, the slug wasn't around much longer for fear of him being served up for dinner. Bon Appetite!

TSgt. Scott Rath, Torrejon AB, Spain
U.S Air Force Firefighter, retired 2004 with 20 years active duty.

JUST THE FACTS

In the deadliest terrorist attack in recent European history, on March 11, 2004, Islamic extremists bombed four commuter trains entering Madrid, causing 191 deaths and over 1,400 injuries.

MECHANICS GONE WILD

Who said that first responders are the only ones with a sense of humor? The following story comes to us from Eric Nielsen, a mechanic for the Los Angeles City Fire Department. He recalls a story he overheard about a group of firefighters, and one poor mechanic, who was in the wrong place, at the wrong time. The story goes that on one particular night, while a group of fire captains were gathered upstairs at a fire station for a meeting with their battalion chief, a number of firefighters and one lone field mechanic assembled downstairs for their own discussion. With a plan hatched, the group of firefighters, along with the single wrench twister stealthily made their way upstairs, huddling together right outside the captain's meeting. They quickly went over their plan to strip down naked, streak across the office space, and then escape out through the other door. All members of the raiding party readied themselves, quickly stripping down to their birthday suits. With everyone ready, the mechanic, who just happened to be in the front of the line, thrust open the office door and burst inside. Unfortunately for him, his fellow nudist forgot to tell him that they weren't coming. They also failed to mention to the bare-all mechanic that they had earlier locked the opposing door, blocking their co-worker's only escape route. When the single streaker made it to the blocked exit, exhilaration quickly turned to panic. With nowhere to go, he simply turned around, and with as much dignity he could muster, calmly walked out the same way he came in, respectfully saluting the captains and the chief along the way.

Erik Nielsen, Mobile Mechanic. Los Angeles City Fire Department. California

CHILD'S PLAY

A lot of kids dream of being a firefighter when they grow up—and some even do… Walking out onto the apparatus floor at his fire station, Captain Thomas Breitsch, of the Euclid Fire Department, came upon some of his crew involved in a bit of horseplay. He wasn't exactly sure what had occurred, but it was very apparent to him that some of his crew were wet, some were angry, and some were laughing hysterically. As this was all unfolding, a young mother and her child walked into the station. She approached Captain Breitsch and asked if her son could see the fire trucks and meet some of the firefighters. She next said, "My son wants to be a firefighter when he grows up." Hearing this, Breitsch quickly turned and looked at his crew, then back at the woman, and replied, "I'm sorry, miss. He needs to make a choice. Does he want to be firefighter or grow up?"

Captain Thomas Breitsch, Euclid Fire Dept. Euclid, Ohio

INFORMATION BULLETIN

FIRE HOUSE DOGS: Dogs were helpful to direct and guard horses during the era of the horse drawn fire engine. Dalmatians were favored probably because of their size, friendly nature, ability to train, and ability to care for themselves. Likewise, urban and nearby departments gave away puppies as new litters were born thus creating an on going fire service tradition.

FREUDIAN SLIP

Now that Trent Sandoval of the City of Henderson Fire Department, Nevada, promoted to engineer, he doesn't get to go inside on calls as much to see what's going on. A few years ago, however, while going through his paramedic internship, Sandoval saw more, or should we say less, than he ever expected. On one particular call, Sandoval and his crew were dispatched to a woman complaining of unusual vaginal bleeding. Being the student, it was Sandoval's responsibility to tend to the patient. He knew all eyes of the two-man rescue/ambulance unit, along with the four-man engine crew would be observing him. Upon entry into the patient's apartment, Sandoval found a near naked 25-year-old woman walking around the apartment wearing only a pair of "thong" underwear. In front of the entire crew and the patient's family, Sandoval nervously worked through the exam, eventually determining that the woman should go with them to the hospital. Noticing that she wasn't wearing any shoes either, the trainee quickly suggested she go slip on a pair of "thongs," meaning shoes. Without missing a beat, the woman's husband, who was nearby, called out, "She already got 'um on!" Hearing this, the entire room burst into laughter, including the patient, allowing Sandoval to slide out of this "Freudian Slip."

Trent Sandoval, Engineer. City of Henderson Fire Department, Nevada

GOOD EVENING

Through training and self discipline, first responders are expected to control their fears and emotions in order to do their sworn duty. First Responders are only human, though, and even the best of them get spooked at one time or another. Richard Janne, a lieutenant with the Sedgwick County Fire District No.1 is no exception. Responding to a late night reported vehicle accident with a possible rollover, Lieutenant Janne found one car down in a ditch, lying on it's top. Grabbing a flashlight and the med kit, Janne headed for the roll over, telling his partner to look for any other possible vehicles involved. Turning his flashlight on, Janne knelt down to look inside the overturned car. He was immediately startled by the site of a man dressed like Dracula, complete with make-up and cape hanging upside down like a bat. In his best Transylvanian accent, Dracula surprised Janne by saying, "Good eeeevening," causing the first responder to quickly jumped back. Dracula then said he was okay, but couldn't get out of the car due to his body weight holding pressure on the seatbelt. At this point, Janne couldn't decide whether he should first help the strangely dressed man or instead drive a wooden stake through the man's heart. Making sure Dracula was flying solo that night, Janne decided he should help the guy out and so he proceeded to free him from the car. Dracula later apologized for scaring Janne. It turns out that Dracula had just returned from work at a local haunted house when he unexpectedly crashed. Happy Halloween—BOO!

Richard Janne, Lieutenant. Sedgwick County Fire District No.1. Wichita, Kansas

IRONIC BEHAVIOR

Sometimes fate has a little irony to it. Arriving on scene of a motor vehicle accident, Paul Pfrimmer, a Firefighter/EMT with New Hanover County Fire Rescue, quickly noticed the severity of the incident. It had started with a van running a stop sign and ended with a semi-truck slamming into its side. With the driver side of the van taking the initial impact, Pfrimmer expected the worse. Surveying the inside of the van, he noticed the semi had penetrated all the way to the middle of the van's cab, demolishing the driver's seat. Luckily, when the collision occurred, the driver was thrown from his seat and landed in the passenger's seat. Even though the collision was traumatic, the driver sustained no injury. A later investigation determined that at the time of the crash, the driver had not been wearing his seatbelt, which ironically saved his life. Pfrimmer found one more ironic thing about the call. Walking around to the back of the van, Pfrimmer chuckled as he read the two bumper stickers that were displayed on the van for all to see. The first one read, "Buckle Up for Safety," the other, "Buckle Up or Eat Glass." Talk about your ironies!

Paul Pfrimmer, Firefighter/EMT. New Hanover County Fire Rescue. Wilmington, North Carolina.

JUST THE FACTS

North Carolina has conducted 13 waves of high visibility enforcement of their seatbelt law since November 1993, and presently has an 84% belt use rate.

Captain David Griffith of the Durham Fire Department, North Carolina has had a long and successful career as a fire officer. Throughout his career he has documented the funny and unusual on-duty events he has encountered by means of skillfully illustrating cartoons. The following cartoon is an example of his work.

How about checking to see if that wheel is on the curb.

A fire apparatus is built and maintained by firefighters to last a long time. We have several reserve pumpers in the city that are 25 to 30 years old. They are used as front line equipment when the newer trucks have to go in for servicing. As the crew of B-shift, Station #1 was backing a 1974 Ward LaFrance into the station, the right front wheel assembly actually fell off of the vehicle. As policy requires, the technician in this illustration was checking with his spotter to make sure he didn't hit anything.

The following four stories were submitted by Norbert Klafta, Captain. (Ret.) Los Angeles City Fire Department, California
Appointed: May 1, 1950 – Retired: November 11, 1975

Career Highlights:
- Authored the pump operator's instruction book for use on the practical portion of the examination for engineer of the fire department.
- First captain assigned to command the hydrant unit.

Notable Incidents Worked:
- La Tuna Canyon and Bel Aire fires
- Watts riot

RIGHT A WRONG

They say history is created by those who write it, however, it doesn't always mean it's correct. January 1953, a heavy downpour of rain had severely weakened a large hillside in the foothills of Los Angeles, California. Los Angeles City Firefighters quickly responded to an emergency call, finding a wooden framed house twisted to a 60-degree angle, sliding down a rain soaked hill. Outside the structure, they found two adults screaming in agony saying their infant child was still inside the house. Without fear for their own well-being, two firefighters raced up the hillside, one losing both his boots in the shin-high mud. Making their way inside the sliding home, they quickly found the baby crying in it's crib. Rescuing the child, they proceeded to slowly inch their way through the muck and debris. Reaching the safety of the street with the baby, they found a police officer who had been directing traffic outside the home. All muddied from the rescue, they quickly handed the baby to him. The next day, a Los Angeles newspaper caption read, "L.A. Cop Saves Child!" Though history may have recorded the facts incorrect, we would now like to right the wrong and give credit where it was truly due: to Firefighter Michael Sullivan and Firefighter Ralph Davis-the true heroes, a job well done!

"Pepe Le Pigeon"

It is a well-known fact that firefighters clean everything around the station; from the kitchen, to the bathroom, even the soot ridden fire hose, which is scrubbed and washed after each and every fire. It is also a fact that this mundane practice of extreme cleanliness can sometimes lead to horseplay. Introducing "Pepe Le Pigeon," the honorary title bestowed upon the person on the receiving end of such mischief. One situation involving Pepe is the hose tower setup. It begins with the routine washing and the scrubbing of the hose, which is then hung evenly to dry vertically from rungs some twenty-five feet high in the hose tower. Pepe is the unlucky firefighter assigned to climb to the top of the tower to position the cleaned hose on the rungs after it's hoisted up. The prank unfolds as the last hose line is raised up secretly connected to a water outlet, and then, just as it reaches Pepe, it's magically charged. The resulting barrage of water soaks the "Pigeon. Now, before you feel sorry for Pepe, just remember, eventually everyone gets his or her turn in the barrel. The mill may grind slow, but exceedingly fine.

Water Sports

In the good old days when things were slow around the fire station, long periods of down time were filled with mischief, mostly involving water. After a playful dousing of a firefighter, this aqueous action usually resulted in an act of revenge. Revenge, however, is said to be a double edge sword. With enough coaxing, a wronged member could be convinced to right things with a good water dousing of the offender. The revengeful firefighter would then position himself high in the station, usually at a second floor window. Armed with a large bucket of water, he would wait patiently for his fellow firefighters to lure the victim in place down below. Unknowingly to the revenge seeker positioned way up high, the not-so helpful crew would inform the victim of what was about to happen. Now duly informed, the intended victim would sneak into the revenge seeker's locker before going outside and put on one of his uniforms. He would then willingly head outside to the target area and get doused. Shortly after the laughter subsided, the bucket dumper would realize he'd been had when he saw his soaking wet uniform hanging on his locker door, causing his thoughts to quickly turn to getting even, twice!

TEMPERAMENTAL CAR

It seems that there is never a lack of amusement around a fire station. One such form of entertainment has earned the nickname "The one up-man-ship." You see, no matter what one did or what one has, someone will always try to better it. One such case of this happened when one engine house firefighter announced a purchase of a high gas mileage economy car. Showing it off to his crew, he boasted proudly about its great fuel economy. After kicking the tires and giving it the once over, the crew congratulated him on his purchase and went about their business—monkey business that is. Always trying to help out a fellow colleague, certain members of the station thought they would try to improve on their friend's good gas mileage by secretly adding extra fuel to the man's car every shift. Unaware of his co-worker's generous gift, the firefighter was astonished with his excellent fuel economy. He continued to sing the car's praises asking himself why he didn't buy this car sooner. His luck, however, was about to change. Just when the firefighter thought his fuel economy couldn't get any better, the same generous firefighters now started siphoning gas back out of the tank. Cheers soon turned to jeers as the same firefighter now exclaimed, "I could get better mileage driving a bus!" Fearing there was something wrong with the vehicle, the firefighter quickly brought his car in for service. The dealership, however, couldn't find anything wrong. This drove the firefighter crazy. The tricksters were not without heart, though. Before the men in the white coats were called, all fuel tampering stopped and things returned to normal. To this day, the practical joke has remained a well-guarded station house secret—that is until now!

Norbert Klafta, Captain (Ret.) Los Angeles City Fire Department, CA.

Captain David Griffith of the Durham Fire Department, North Carolina has had a long and successful career as a fire officer. Throughout his career he has documented the funny and unusual on-duty events he has encountered by means of skillfully illustrating cartoons. The following cartoon is an example of his work.

I don't care if the world is on fire.... I'm going to the third floor!

Fire crews responded to an all too common automatic fire alarm in an assisted living high rise downtown. As several crews loaded into the elevator to investigate the problem on the upper floors, one of the residents of the facility thought there was room on the elevator for her.

MAKE MINE DECAF

Everyone's familiar with the old family remedy of treating a cold with grandma's chicken soup. In Los Angeles, California, however, some unscrupulous residents have come up with their own treatment for what ails them. Responding to a reported overdose call, Firefighter Robert Besch, of the Los Angeles City Fire Department, and a paramedic crew entered a house to find an unconscious man lying on the ground, not breathing. Surrounding the patient stood two women, whom at the time seemed somewhat puzzled. Seeing the tell-tale signs of the type of call they were on, Besch and the paramedics went to work on the patient, treating him with the appropriate medication. As they did, they could hear the two women in the background mumbling, "I don't know why it's not working!" Luckily, a few minutes later the paramedic's medication kicked in, and the unconscious man started breathing on his own. Besch walked over to the two women and asked them what had happened. The women explained to him that the man had passed out after taking heroin and that they had given him a shot of coffee to wake him up. Firefighter Besch then tried to explain to the women that they should never give anything by mouth to an unconscious patient. In their defense, the women quickly answered back, "Oh no, we didn't give him anything by mouth. We took the needles we were using and injected him with coffee, but it didn't work. It must have been decaf!"

Engineer Robert Besch, Los Angeles City Fire Department. California

PITCHER'S PRIDE

You may be able to peel a piece of gum off the bottom of your shoe, but a nickname will stick with you forever. Bob Pitcher, a firefighter with Smithfield Fire Department in Utah, found this out the hard way, literally. Responding to a reported overdose call, Pitcher and his fire company arrived at a residence to find a patient in respiratory distress. Recognizing the seriousness of the situation, Pitcher quickly started breathing for the patient using an Ambu bag for ventilations as the EMT-Intermediate started an IV. When the paramedic unit arrived on scene, Pitcher watched as they administered a dose of Narcan, a medication that reverses the effects of opium type drugs. A short time passed, and the patient's respirations started to improve. One paramedic then asked Pitcher if he would please switch the patient over to a non-rebreather oxygen mask. Doing as requested, Firefighter Pitcher started switching the tubing from the oxygen tank. As he did, the metal tank suddenly tipped over, striking the semi-conscious patient just above the right eye, causing him to moan in pain. Luckily, there was no harm done... except to Pitcher's pride. Not long after the call, Firefighter Pitcher was honored with the long standing tradition of receiving a nickname. To this day, he is affectionately known to his friends as "BONK!"

Robert Pitcher, Firefighter. Smithfield Fire Department, North Smithfield, Utah

THE MAKING OF A FIRE DEPARTMENT

A Poem

Take some men that yesterday were boys,
Give them hose and ladders to replace their toys.

Recruit and train from a wide diversity,
And instill a solid camaraderie.

The ingredients are there, the mixture is right.
Let the training begin show them how to fight.

Fire is the enemy whenever it appears.
It's an ongoing battle been 'round for years.

We train men and women, with dedication and hope.
The ones that apply themselves study and promote.

Out of the field and downtown they go.
They're the ones now leading the show.

Decisions are different learning is too,
Discovering things they never knew.

Enforcing the rules and taking command,
Promoting good will whenever they can.

You're the heroes of today and it's up to you,
As you do your job and see it through.

Remember, the goal you have is mighty fine,
"TO PRESERVE LIFE AND PROPERTY"
...Is your gift to mankind.

Written 1987 by Bernadette Pelletier, Los Angeles City Fire Department,
Firefighter / Paramedic II. California

JUST THE FACTS

Livermore Fire Department, California —"Centennial Light." A hand-blown, four-watt bulb with a carbon filament made by the Shelby Electric Company, is reported to be the nation's longest burning light bulb. The bulb was donated to the fire department in 1901 by Dennis Bernal who owned the Livermore Power and Light Company. It was first installed at the fire department house cart house in 1901. It was left burning continuously as a nightlight over the fire trucks for over 100 years. In 1972 *Ripley's Believe-It-or-Not* researched it and declared it the oldest known working light bulb. The light has also been declared the oldest known working light bulb by the *Guinness Book of World Records*. **www.Centennialbulb.org**

"TRIBUTE TO OUR FALLEN"

By retired Captain Paul Beckingham, 24-year Veteran of the Toronto Fire Service, Canada.

www.firescapes.ca - for Firefighter / Paramedic art in oils, pen, ink, and tattoo art.

SECONDS ANYONE!

Most people are under the impression that all firefighters are good cooks. That, however, is just like saying all Californians look like movie stars. The truth is, even the fire service has its share of culinary challenged people. One fine example of this is a firefighter we'll call Sam. One day Sam was asked to cook lunch. Knowing his own limitations, he decided to keep it simple and prepared tuna fish sandwiches for his crew. Everything started out fine as Sam quickly gathered the necessary ingredients. One main element was missing, though—mayonnaise. "No problem," thought Sam. "I'll just find something else to add to the tuna." Noontime came and the rest of the fire crew sat down to enjoy lunch. With great anticipation, Sam's fellow firefighters dug in, only to have to spit it out seconds later. "Are you trying to kill us?" One firefighter quickly exclaimed. "What's in this stuff?" Surprised at their reaction, Sam answered, "Well, I ran out of mayonnaise, so I substituted it with Crisco instead. What's the problem?" Let's just say—Sam has been permanently removed from the cooking rotation.

John Hicks, Firefighter / Paramedic. Los Angeles City Fire Department, California

JUST THE FACTS

George W. Bright, hired October 2, 1897, was the first black member of the Los Angeles Fire Department.

Over the years, the public has shown their gratitude towards first responders for the dangerous work they do. What most don't know, however, is that without a support staff of people behind the scenes, all of the heroic stuff accomplished by the first responders would be virtually impossible. We're talking about the unsung heroes of the departments: the mechanics, painters, electricians, and all the other support staff that help first responders do their job safer, smarter, and sometimes in a better environment. The following stories come from one such hero, Ray Jordan, a civilian electrician for the City of Los Angeles. Over the years, he has had the opportunity to witness first hand the playful side of first responders as evident in the following stories.

PULLING THE CAPTAIN'S CHAIN

While crawling through the attic of a fire station to pull wires for a new computer system, Jordan discovered a heavy piece of chain, some six feet in length, with a light piece of cord tied to each end. Not being able to see where the opposite ends of the cords went, he asked one of the firefighters about the mysterious chain. Immediately, the firefighter hushed him, looking around the apparatus floor suspiciously. When he saw that the coast was clear, the firefighter then proceeded to explain to him in a low tone that the chain ran directly over the captain's dorm, and that every night, right before the captain fell asleep, someone would pull the cord hard enough to cause the chain to scrape across the attic, rattling the captain's nerves. Each shift, the jokesters would pull the opposite end of the cord, causing similar results. This antic went on for some time, the captain never being the wiser.

I Can't See Getting Seconds

Another story Jordan can remember, occurred one afternoon when he joined a crew of firefighters for lunch. On the menu that day was "Eyeball Stew," a mixture of small, new potatoes, cooked meat, and assortments of fresh vegetables, all mixed in a large, cast iron pot. This particular dish received its name from the small potatoes that resembled eyeballs. Not being able to pass on a golden opportunity, one mischievous firefighter thought he would be funny and add his own particular ingredient to the meal. Securing a real cow's eye from a local slaughterhouse the day before, this particular individual waited until everyone served up their first helping of stew, then, when no one was looking, he plopped the globe in the middle of the pot, the single pupil staring upward for all to see. Let's just say that after discovering the special ingredient, no one could "see" getting seconds.

JUST THE FACTS

The first cow in America arrived in Jamestown colony in 1611. Until the 1850's, nearly every family had its own cow.

The first regular shipment of milk by railroad was between Orange County, New York, and New York City and began in 1841.

ROOKIE'S REVENGE

Electrician, Ray Jordan shares another story. During dinner at a Los Angeles City Fire Station, he was witness to how far a firefighter will go to get a good laugh. While enjoying a nice spaghetti dinner, a senior firefighter walked in and sat across from a rookie. Without warning, the senior member starting pulling a long piece of spaghetti out of his nose which he had hidden in its hiding place prior to entering the kitchen. Seeing this grotesque act, the rookie immediately turned a light shade of green. All in attendance started laughing. The rookie, however, would have the last laugh.   Seconds later, he returned the sickening act with one of his own, throwing up all over the table, and ruining everyone's meal.

Ray Jordan, Electrician. (Ret.) City of Los Angeles, California

JUST THE FACTS

The First industrial pasta factory in America was built in Brooklyn in 1848 by, of all people, a Frenchman, who spread his spaghetti strands on the roof to dry in the sunshine.

SORRY CHIEF

Have you ever been in the wrong place at the right time? Well, I can tell you of at least one company of first responders that has been. One morning at a structure fire, a rescue company was given orders to take out the windows in the rear of the structure to ventilate the building. At the same time, other firefighters were setting up equipment and advancing hose into the front of the structure. As they did, they were surprised to hear the breaking and crashing of glass from behind them. Unfortunately, the rescue company had mistakenly broken out the windows of the wrong building, almost giving a heart attack to an older gentleman as he sat inside reading the morning paper. Needless to say the fire chief was not a happy camper that morning!

John Hudak, Driver-Engineer. Florida

JUST THE FACTS

During the 1991 Gulf War, the busiest military port in the country was Jacksonville, Florida. From this location, the military moved more supplies and people than any other port in the country.

HISTORY OF THE MALTESE CROSS

The badge of a firefighter is the Maltese Cross. The Maltese Cross is a symbol of protection and a badge of honor. Its story is hundreds of years old. When a courageous band of crusaders known as "The Knights of St. John" fought the Saracens for possession of the holy land, they encountered a new weapon unknown to European warriors. It was a simple, but horrible device of war. It brought excruciating pain and agonizing death upon the brave fighters for the cross. As the crusaders advanced on the walls of the city, they were struck by glass bombs containing naphtha. When they became saturated with the highly flammable liquid, the Saracens would hurl a flaming torch into their midst. Hundreds of the knights were burned alive; others risked their lives to save their brothers-in-arms from dying painful, fiery deaths. Thus, these men became our first firefighters and the first of a long list of courageous men. Their heroic efforts were recognized by fellow crusaders who awarded each hero a badge of honor - a cross similar to the one firefighters wear today. Since the Knights of St. John lived on a little island in the Mediterranean Sea named Malta, the cross came to be known as the Maltese Cross. The Maltese Cross is our symbol of protection. It means that the firefighter who wears this cross is willing to lay down his life for you just as the crusaders sacrificed their lives for their fellow man so many years ago. The Maltese Cross is a firefighter's badge of honor, signifying that he works in courage - a ladder's rung away from death.

50,000 VOLTS OF REVENGE

The M26 Taser device is a common law enforcement tool. The device is intended for use as a less-lethal force option. Looking much like an officer's service weapon, the laser-sited device uses cartridges attached to the end of the barrel. The cartridges propel a pair of darts on copper wires up to 21 feet. Upon contact with the suspect, the device can send 50,000 volts of electricity over the copper wires in a five-second cycle, overriding the target's motor and sensory systems. Without the cartridge, the tazer can also function as a contact stun device. Although this is a useful tool in the hands of a competent law enforcement officer, some-times, "Stupid is as stupid does!" Sam Hanna, a firefighter with Los Palomas Fire/Rescue in Southern New Mexico, overheard the following story while working at the local sheriff's office during a school-to-work program in high school. The story goes that while a number of deputies were standing around outside the sheriff's office engaged in conversa-tion, one of the deputies noticed a spider crawling across the windshield of his unit. The deputy leaned over the car, bracing himself by holding onto the metal windshield frame. He then pressed the stun points of his M26 Taser against the windshield in an attempt to fry the spider. When the deputy triggered the device, however, the 50,000 volts of elec-tricity not only succeeded in terminating the spider, but it also surged through the vehicle right back into the unsuspecting deputy. Lucky for him, the other deputies assisted him off the vehicle, a little bit stunned, but hopefully a little smarter!

Sam Hanna, Firefighter, Los Palomas Fire/Rescue. Williamsburg, New Mexico

ZEROES TO HEROES

As a first responder, you must always be careful of what you say and who is around when you say it. Receiving a call of a woman stuck in a chimney, Lieutenant Jeff Eschenburg and his Engine 16 crew from the City of Albuquerque Fire Department, New Mexico, arrived on scene of a single family home. While his crew laddered the building, Eschenburg enter the residence to investigate. Looking up the flue of the chimney, he quickly spotted a young lady's foot hanging down just beyond the flue trap. Luckily, the woman was not hurt, only scared. Eschenburg next made his way up to the roof to get a better view of the situation. Once there, he could see the soot-covered woman down in the chimney just out of arms reach of her rescuers. Meanwhile, the rescue officer on scene called for their heavy technical rescue crew. This action disturbed Eschenburg and his crew because it would mean a longer time at the incident, and it also reflected badly on them, insinuating they couldn't handle the situation. When the technical rescue crew arrived at the rooftop, Eschenburg asked them to manage the ground sector while his team of firefighters went to work on the problem up above. Rejecting an idea to breakdown the chimney stack, one of Eschenburg's crew members, Firefighter Kevin Loghry, convinced the trapped girl to start moving around, which eventually freed her at the shoulders. Another crew member, Firefighter Josh Munson, then pulled a five-foot piece of webbing from his bunkers and lowered it down to the girl. With the girl managing to grab it, the firefighters then pulled her up to safety. The girl was covered in soot and a little embarrassed, but uninjured. Suddenly from the roof top, Munson yelled out, *"Cancel the heroes, she was saved by the zeroes!"* After the rescue, Eschenburg asked the girl and her boyfriend about their thought process behind the decision for her to enter the chimney. The boyfriend answered that he had coaxed his girlfriend to climb down the chimney after she inadvertently locked her keys in the house. During their conversation, Eschenburg humorously brought up Santa Clause, and asked them if they really thought he could come down the chimney without his "Magic Dust?" The next day, Eschenburg paid the price for his Santa Clause statement when he was misquoted in a local newspaper, the column leaving out the "Magic Dust" statement. Needless to say, he caught a little flack from the fire personnel from the surrounding stations for ruining for all the little kids the mystique that Santa Clause could not come down the chimney. (Don't worry, Lieutenant, we still believe!)

Engine 16-A Jeff Eschenburg, Lieutenant. Josh Munson, Firefighter. Kevin Lohgry, Firefighter. City of Albuquerque Fire Department, New Mexico

JUST THE FACTS

In 1950, the little cub that was to become the National Fire Safety symbol, Smokey the Bear, was found trapped in a tree when his home in Lincoln National Forest was destroyed by fire. In 1963, in Smokey's honor, the New Mexican legislature chose the black bear to be the official state animal.

A TRUCK AND A PRAYER

Through his many years of service with the Vail Fire and Emergency Services, located in the State of Colorado, Captain Jim Spell has seen his fair share of horrendous vehicle accidents. Luckily, as his career progressed, so did the advances in highway safety, effectively reducing the number of highway fatalities. There was one accident, however, that happened earlier in his career that would bring any seasoned veteran to his knees, or at least two civilians. It was 1981 when Spell was newly promoted to fire technician. Being full of spunk, the young driver couldn't wait to receive the next call for help. Not that he wished any harm to come anyone, but if it was going to happen, Spell wanted to be the one there practicing his newly acquired training of saving lives. He would soon get that chance as he heard the voice of the dispatcher call out, "Attention Vail officers on duty, we have a report of a runaway semi-truck, westbound I-70, mile marker 185, estimated speed of over 100 miles per hour." Seeing the possibility of death and destruction in his mind, Spell and his resident firefighter saddled up and headed out towards the pass. Having a motor governor installed on his truck was probably a good thing at the time, since Spell's adrenaline level was now heading towards his internal redline. Figuring the semi would head for a newly installed runaway ramp, which was a section of road graded on an incline filled with sand to stop runaway trucks, Spell and his partner headed in that direction. Arriving on scene, the two men quickly discovered a semi-tractor and trailer stuck halfway up the safety incline with smoke and steam billowing from it. As Spell inched his truck closer to the runaway ramp he feared the worse, spotting two bodies up against the front wheel well. Seeing this surreal scene, Spell parked the fire truck at the bottom of the ramp, grabbed his medical kit and oxygen tank, and headed for the victims. As he raced passed the smoking trailer, he soon came upon the two victims kneeling near the front tire of the semi-truck. Halting at the first man, a gray-haired old gentleman, Spell bent

down to check his condition. Suddenly, the old man turned towards Spell and said, "Just a minute, friend. If you will please excuse us just a moment, me and my son would like to finish praying. Thank you."

(Both of the vehicle's occupants were fine.)

James G. Spell, Captain. Vail Fire and Emergency Services, Colorado

JUST THE FACTS

As of 2005, Pueblo, Colorado, is the only city in America with four living recipients of the Medal of Honor.

STRESSFUL REACTION

John Allan was a career firefighter in the United States Air Force. Now retired, Allan finished up his long and successful career as the Fire Chief at RAF Woodbridge Base in the United Kingdom. As a veteran firefighter, he became acutely aware of how stress can impact job performance, as illustrated in the following story. In the early part of his career (1973), Allan, a master sergeant at the time, was stationed at Elmendorf AFB, Alaska. One day his fire company responded to the base housing area for a residential basement fire. Upon arrival, the crew found the basement of one of the homes fully involved, but contained. Allan was the driver operator of the first-in engine and his crew immediately went to work advancing hose lines to the stair entrance. Next on scene was the truck company that was given the instructions to ventilate the basement via windows on the opposite side of the attack. Two young firefighters took their axes and headed into position. When the signal was given to take out the windows, one of the firefighters laid down his axe, took off his gloves, and smashed the window out with his bare hand. Later in the hospital, while getting the back of his hand stitched up, Allan asked him why he took off his gloves. The young firefighter answered that at the time of the incident he didn't recall thinking about it. This proves that stress can affect people in many ways.

John Allan, USAF Master Sergeant (Ret.) / CFPS / Fire Protection Engineer, Elmendorf AFB, Alaska.

THE DEFINITION OF A VOLUNTEER

The definition of a volunteer is one who enters into, or offers himself for service of his own free will. In the fire service, this usually means get the rookie to do it. Responding to a report of a bomb inside the local high school, the Lee County Sheriffs Department from Opelika, Alabama, requested additional help from the local fire service to search the building. Wanting to show their worth, and knowing they didn't have much of a choice anyway, two rookie firefighters from the Friendship Firefighter Association volunteered for the dangerous detail. Beginning the hazardous bomb search, one of the rookie firefighters entered the boy's lavatory. Dead silence filled the air as the junior member began his search of the bathroom, slowly crawling on his hands and knees looking for the bomb. With his heart rate already soaring, he passed by one of the open stalls, inadvertently activating the motion sensitive automatic toilet. The explosive rush of flushing water sent a shockwave of impending doom through the rookie's soul making it now a necessity, rather than a duty, to occupy the bathroom. Minutes later and a few pounds lighter, he emerged from the room, pale and sweaty, and thinking twice about volunteering for anything in the future that could go "Boom!"

Angelia Richards, Deputy Chief. Friendship Firefighters Association, Alabama

CANCEL THE REPAIR

One morning, Firefighter Kent Mallette and his crew were called out to a single car accident in Broken Bow, Nebraska. Upon arrival on scene, Mallette observed two sheriff deputies talking to a middle-aged executive type man, standing next to his white 1997 BMW. The car was at rest in a pasture after going off the highway and through a fence. The driver was okay and refused transport. The firefighters had the driver sign the mandatory refusal form and then headed back to the station. On the drive back, the fire crew heard a deputy still on scene, broadcast, "Dispatch. Will you contact Miracle Dent (a local body shop) and advise them that their white 97 BMW appointment will not be there this morning."

Kent Mallette, Emergency Services Director. Broken Bow, Nebraska.

INFORMATION BULLETIN

The blue background field on the American flag is called the "Union" or "Canton."

EMS

THE HUMAN TOUCH

In the EMS community, it is easy to lose yourself and the feelings that we should hold towards the patients we treat. We sometimes act as if it is just like any other job, treating our patients as simply customers. However, the career of saving lives is much more than just a simple job, and our patients are not just customers; they are people. People with real emotions, and feelings, needing the same thing we all need—the human touch. In the following story, EMS Division Chief Randy J. James reminds us that we are more than just public servants doing a job—we are human beings, too!

Recently, Chief James wrote us about an event that brought his EMS career back into focus, reminding himself of one of his strongholds in the world of EMS after 26 years. This stronghold had nothing to do with needles, or dosages of medicine, or squiggly little lines running across a heart monitor. It simply had to do with the gentle soul of a little old lady with a minor request—a request to hold her hand. As James took her outreached hand, he quickly pondered if he should ask the twenty health questions that he did of all his patients. Was her range of motion decreased? Probably not, he determined; she could move her arm over to take his hand. Was she suffering from weakness? Paralysis? He guessed not; she had a good, strong grip. Did she need breathing medicines? He guessed not; she was moving enough good air in and out and had a steadiness in her voice as she asked him to hold her hand all the way to the hospital. This made him think that he would rather have his hands removed with a chainsaw than to forego this precious and powerful gift of touch.

On the way to the hospital, he listened as she told him her entire history, not medical history, but life history. They arrived at the hospital some thirty-minutes later. At this point, the thought of getting a second set of vitals per protocol was as important to him as watching rust form on metal. He knew that he wasn't neglecting her medical needs, as the

142

human touch was the best medicine at the time. All he could now think about was how great of an impact the woman's request for human touch had on him. It made him wonder if his EMS career had now come full circle. Chief James remembered back to the time when he had made up his mind to take the next step in his career/life and become a full fledged medic. He had known that in the past he had shortchanged his patients by not being fully trained. Not that he had been harming them, but rather, he realized they needed more than he was able to give at the time and certainly more than the twenty health questions he asked. Government regulations won't permit us to reveal the patient's name, but Chief James would like to acknowledge and thank her for helping him realize that the human touch was mightier than the monitor, mightier than the needle, and mightier than any drug he carried.

Randy J. James, EMS Division Chief. Jackson Township Fire Department, Indiana

JUST THE FACTS

In 1934 Chicago Gangster John Dillinger escaped the Lake Country Jail in Crown Point, Indiana, by using a "pistol" he had carved from a wooden block.

A CHORUS OF LAUGHTER

First responders are notorious for not getting enough sleep, quickly turning them into tall two year olds. Mauri "Mo" Simonds, a Crew Chief/EMT with Colchester Rescue, located in the beautiful state of Vermont, knows humor is one way to keep her weary crew alert. After a particularly exhausting day on weekend duty, Mo was stashing her worn jumpsuit into her locker when tones sounded. Jumping back into uniform, Mo and the crew dashed to the truck and headed out to the call. Arriving on scene of a senile elderly woman, Mo attempted to decipher the laundry list of complaints from her patient. Figuring out what health problem needed immediate attention, Mo began her transport of the woman. During the transportation, the not so seriously ill patient began serenading the crew with a repertoire of songs in her head. Offering her levity to the situation, Mo began shouting over the ringing of the woman's obvious malfunctioning hearing aid. Seeing that she had her attention, Mo said, "Ma'am, I want to tell you something. This is our driver's first time driving an ambulance. He used to drive garbage trucks, but he came to us yesterday and told us he wanted to drive our big, white ambulances." Hearing this, the woman's face lit up, and she squealed in delight, enthusiastically saying, "Well, he's doing a fine job!" Arriving at the hospital, Mo and her crew started unloading the patient. As the driver (who really had a number of years behind the wheel of the ambulance) came around to assist them, the elderly woman reached out for him and gently took his hand and spoke, "Son, you made an excellent decision—save the trash, don't dump it." Unaware of the earlier comments, the confused driver just nodded and smiled, causing the rest of the crew to dissolve into a concert of laughter.

Mauri "Mo" Simonds, Crew Chief/EMT. Colchester Rescue, Vermont

AMBULANCE 101

While working as a paramedic on an ambulance in a fairly large Indiana city, Jim Perkins and his crew were called out to the local college for a seizure. Upon their arrival to the dorm room of a young male in his early twenties, they found him in his bed just coming out of a grand mal seizure. After all of the appropriate on scene treatment—the usual oxygen, IV, and heart monitor—they loaded him onto the cot and started to transport him out to the awaiting ambulance. As they wheeled him down the hallway, he began to wake up. To his alarm, he found himself on a moving bed and surrounded by strangers. Since there were about ten first responders, including all of the firemen and ambulance personnel, he was very frightened, asking, "Who are you people?" Perkins replied to him that they were paramedics and firemen and that they were here to help him because he had just suffered a seizure. The patient then asked, "What's going on?" From the back of the crowd, a fireman called out, "Ambulance 101." Without hesitation the patient quickly replied, "Please take me by the admissions office on the way out." When asked why, he then replied, "Because I'm dropping this class!"

Jamey Perkins, Paramedic. Brazil, Indiana

Jamey Perkins is an experienced paramedic with more than fifteen years in the emergency medical field. He currently owns a web designing, web site hosting, and domain services business found at: **www.siteexpressions.com.**

145

GALLOWS HUMOR

One morning, EMS Lieutenant Dale Briggs of the Bristol Fire Department responded with his crew to a fatal car crash which terminated in a creek. It appeared that the car had been traveling at a high rate of speed when it hit a slight depression in the road causing it to become airborne. The vehicle bent the curved steel bridge railing and took out a cement support holding the railing. The car then crashed through the metal barrier, winding upside down in the water below. One victim was half out of the water, lying D.O.A. on the bank of the creek. Sometime later, the car was pulled from the water revealing yet another victim inside. With Bristol Fire being a rural volunteer fire department, a private ambulance was called to transport the deceased. It took approximately 30 minutes for the ambulance to arrive for the first fatality. The second ambulance, however, was still not there after more than an hour. As they were waiting for the second ambulance to arrive, one of the younger EMT's suggested that they simply stand the "stiff" up on a nearby tree and pin a note to his chest reading "Take Me!"

Now before you think this is inappropriate humor, please take the following into consideration. If you had ever watched the television show M*A*S*H, you would know how important humor therapy is to relieving stress. In that TV series, the characters used a style of humor that made light of tragedy, suffering, and death, which is called "gallows humor." This type of humor is regarded as a critical stress balancing tactic and can help first responders cope with exposure to horror and to make the best of what can't be changed. Even though this type of humor is beneficial for first responders, its use must be kept in-house— meaning only for the first responders involved in the incident. It is not intended for others, such as patients, family, and friends, who might not understand the use of this humor and misinterpret it as cruel, uncaring, and disrespectful. The above story illustrates the appropriate use of "gallows humor" as a self-care technique, allowing the first

146

responders on scene to convert their unpleasant or depressed feelings into a more agreeable mindset in order to deal with the tragedy.

EMS Lt. Dale Briggs. Bristol Fire Department. Bloomfield, Ohio

JUST THE FACTS

1952: Marshal Dotson "pop" Sutton of Ohio, age 80, becomes the oldest officer to die in the line of duty.

EMS HEALTH SAFETY TIP

STROKE—Sometimes the symptoms of a stroke are difficult to identify. Unfortunately, the lack of awareness spells disaster. The stroke victim may suffer brain damage when people nearby fail to recognize the symptoms of a stroke. Now doctors say any bystander can recognize a stroke by asking three simple questions:

- Ask the individual to smile.

- Ask him or her to raise both arms.

- Ask the person to speak a simple sentence.

If he or she has trouble with any of these tasks, call 9-1-1, immediately and describe the symptoms to the dispatcher.

DOG DAY AFTERNOON

Back in the late 1970's, High Noon, Saturday… Jim Freeman, a paramedic for McGann Ambulance providing contracted ALS service for St. Joseph County, Indiana, was cruising the streets of a Midwest town in his Type I Ambulance in search of a fast food fix. Occupying the ambulance with him was his partner, John, the second medic riding in the back, and Art, an EMT who was driving. With all eyes searching for a place to eat, they suddenly encountered an elderly woman standing on the sidewalk, yelling for help. Pulling over to offer their assistance, the three men heard the woman screaming, "Help, my dog!" Giving the immediate area a closer look, the three men observed two dogs on the sidewalk caught in a compromising position, showing no signs of distress. The woman on the other hand was a different story. Wanting to calm her nerves, John jumped out of the back of the ambulance apparently aware that cold water would remedy the situation. With a large bottle of sterile water, the EMT began chasing the dogs down the street while starting the baptism process. Thinking the whole ordeal must have been quite a sight for curious onlookers, Jim and Art remained in the ambulance, unable to contain their laughter.

Jim Freeman, Paramedic. McGann Ambulance. South Bend, Indiana

JUST THE FACTS

You're more likely to get stung by a bee on a windy day than in any other weather.

FORGET ME NOT?

Forgot where you placed your car keys? Forgot where you placed your glasses? Can't remember the phone number to 911—maybe it's stress! Station Supervisor Tom Veatch of American Medical Response located on the island of Kauai, Hawaii, knows this to be true. Encountering the reporting party at her residence concerning her ill child, Paramedic Veatch learned that the woman had originally called the fire station where her husband worked as a firefighter relaying that under the stress of the moment "she had forgotten the number to 911." To say the least, the firefighter/husband was embarrassed. Thankfully, everything turned out okay. Stress Happens!

Tom Veatch, MICT (Mobile Intensive Care Technician). Kauai, Hawaii

Tom is a member of the International Affiliation of Theatrical and Stage Employees, Local #665, where he works as a set medic. Tom has also been appointed to two consecutive four year terms on the Hawaii Governor's EMS Advisory Committee (EMSAC)

Why does Hawaii have Interstates?

HUMILITY

Inclined to be an EMT,
I signed up for the class.
I thought the course might be intense
But knew that I could pass.

I filled out forms for this and that
Until my arm was tired.
Proof of shots and illnesses
For this course was required.

They said I would need to find
Records from childhood days.
Locating what they wanted, though,
Turned into quite a maze.

Records thought to be at home
Were either lost or burnt.
I looked where I had thought they were
But found they really weren't.

I called my elementary school
But files had been destroyed.
I called the county office next
But they just seemed annoyed.

I went and asked my instructor
If there were other ways
To generate the records from
My early, by gone days.

(Now understand my quandary:
My age was near two score,
I'd had a wife for sixteen years,
My children numbered four.)

He had a little impish grin
As he explained another.
To meet the demands of the class
I'd need a note from Mother!

Darryl Claassen, Chief. Whitewater River Fire District. Whitewater, Kansas

JUST THE FACTS

Fire Station No. 4 in Lawrence, Kansas, originally a stone barn constructed in 1858, was a station site on the Underground Railroad.

151

RADIO BABBLE

Over the years, Rita Herrington, a RN/EMT-P located in Bloomington, Indiana, has heard her share of humorous patient reports over the Indiana Hospital Emergency Radio Network (IHERN). Here are a few of her favorites.

While giving a patient report over the radio, one excited EMT stated, "The girl got her car caught in the finger door!"

Another comical anecdote involves an EMT that had assured the emergency room staff that all was well because the patient was immobilized with "sea bags and sand collars."

One new EMT using 10 codes for communication mistakenly called in a riot, instead of a psychiatric patient as intended. This caused the emergency room staff to persistently call the bewildered rookie medic inquiring how many patients were arriving.

Lastly, she retells the story of one IHERN transmission reporting to dispatch that the ambulance was transporting "one female patient and one female mother."

Rita Herrington, RN/EMT-P. Bloomington, Indiana

JUST THE FACTS

Research indicates that mosquitoes are attracted to people who have recently eaten bananas.

Captain David Griffith of the Durham Fire Department, North Carolina has had a long and successful career as a fire officer. Throughout his career he has documented the funny and unusual on-duty events he has encountered by means of skillfully illustrating cartoons. The following cartoon is an example of his work.

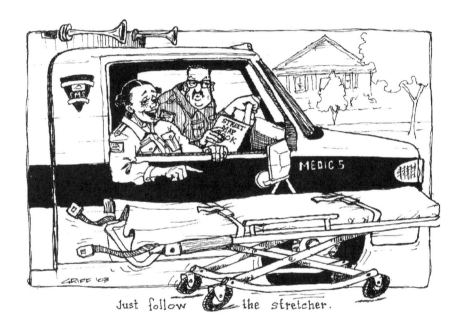

Just follow the stretcher.

Medic 5 of the County EMS shares the station with Engine 5 of the City department. Shortly after shift change, they got a call and sped out of the station. They forgot that the rear doors were still open and the stretcher was unsecured as they were still checking out equipment for their tour of duty for the night. The stretcher never made it to the call.

TIME IS OF THE ESSENCE

The personnel of the Henderson Fire Department provide their customers with the highest level of service possible. They are always professional, skilled, and quick to respond to their calls. Working on an ambulance, Firefighter Israel Wilkinson and his partner promptly responded to a call for CPR in progress. They arrived on scene to find a patient slumped over on a front porch with a man (his neighbor) pounding on his chest. The neighbor was extremely panicked as he vigorously preformed CPR on the victim. As Firefighter Wilkinson knelt down to take over CPR, he heard a strange sound emanating from the victim every time the neighbor did a chest compression. He also noticed the victim's eyes were halfway open, and he could hear him mumbling "ouch" every time his chest was pushed. Seeing this, the firefighters quickly asked the neighbor to step to the side so they could assess the patient. Upon finishing their exam, they quickly diagnosed that the patient had low blood sugar, which caused him to appear unconscious to the untrained eye. In reality, however, the patient was only in a state of insulin shock and was still able to respond to voice or pain stimulus. After treating the patient, Wilkinson tried to calm down the concerned neighbor. Not wanting to discourage the man's good intentions, but still wanting to educate him, Wilkinson told the neighbor that essentially one needs a dead person before CPR can be performed. Wilkinson then told him he had good technique but asked him if he had checked for a pulse. Quite frustrated with the question, and still excited about the rescue he had just performed, the neighbor wildly gestured as he exploded, "I didn't have time!"

Israel Wilkinson, Firefighter, Henderson Fire Department, Nevada

154

NAKED THERAPY

Some people believe first responders are immune from the terrible things they witness, enabling them to go about their daily duties as if they were a common chore. This, however, couldn't be further from the truth. Everyone needs something to help him or her decompress. Under stress, your sense of humor is one of the first things to go. But if you can laugh at the situation, you'll be amazed at how much better you feel. Frances Kibbe, an EMT-B from a Massachusetts Ambulance Company, uses one such example of this therapy. Looking back, she recalls the time she responded to the state police barracks for an unknown medical complaint. There, she discovered a young female sitting calmly and in no obvious distress. Witnesses had stated that the patient, for unknown reasons, had earlier flipped out at a local gas station, screaming and yelling at the clerk. Hoping the patient's current docile behavior would continue, EMT Kibbe started her examination. Kibbe's hope soon ran out, though, as the patient again went on her emotional outburst, threatening to punch and kick anyone near. With things soon calmed, EMT Kibbe, along with another first responder, started their transport to the local hospital. Arriving at the E.R. without incident, Kibbe quickly turned over care of the patient and headed for a private room to start her paperwork. Suddenly, commotion broke out in the hall. From a back room, Kibbe stuck her head out, witnessing the female patient she had just transported, running down the corridor as naked as the first day she was born, three large guards in hot pursuit. Ducking back into the safety of her little niche, Kibbe next heard a loud thud, followed by the long squeaking sound of bare skin sliding across the floor. All Frances Kibbe could think about is how much that must have hurt. Using humor, however, allowed her to move from the grim and bare it, to the grin and share it.

Frances Kibbe, EMT. Massachusetts

SHOCKING RESULTS

We have all witnessed the familiar scene on television: the one set in an emergency room, a young, good-looking doctor standing over a pulse-less patient with a pair of large defibrillator paddles firmly gripped in his hands yelling, "All clear!" In TV land, it seems so simple and without complications, however, as paramedic first responders know, life doesn't always imitate art. The following story is a fine example of this. While on duty in the beginning stage of his career, Marty Johnson, a paramedic from Missouri, reported to a man down call. Arriving on scene, he found an elderly patient, pulse-less, and not breathing, with family members performing CPR. Reacting as he was trained, Johnson cut open the front of the patient's shirt, exposing the man's bare chest. Quickly determining that the patient was in ventricular fibrillation, Johnson next placed the paddles on the correct anatomical landmarks and defibrillated the patient twice. Now if this were a scene from a television show, this would be the part where the camera would pan to the heart monitor, showing a normal beating heart. Unfortunately, this was not Hollywood. Prior to defibrillating the patient, Paramedic Johnson had forgotten to apply the conductive jell to the paddles. The resulting electrical arc ignited the patient's shirt, starting it on fire. Calls of panic quickly emanated from the patient's family standing behind Johnson, one person screaming, "They're burning Daddy!" With smoke rising and tempers flaring, the patient's family quickly turned against the paramedics causing an ensuing fight to break out between them. With anarchy erupting, the police soon arrived, ending this non-Hollywood type story!

Marty Johnson, Paramedic. Missouri

THE MORNING SHOW

Robin Bobay, an EMS Captain with the Northeast Allen County Fire and EMS is not against her crew watching television on duty, she just doesn't like it while they work on patients. Called out on an early morning run to a reported 67-year-old male having chest pain, Bobay arrived on scene in her personal vehicle at the same time as her BLS crew and a paramedic team. Entering the house, the first responders went to work, quickly taking vital signs. Bobay soon began to observe her crew diverting their attention from the patient to the television in the room. With smirks on their faces, the entire first responder team stood there, watching the television. Noticing the first responders growing interest on what was on the television, the patient angrily yelled for his wife to find the television remote so he could turn it off. Turning towards the TV, Bobay caught a glimpse of what her crew was so mesmerized with. Flashing across the screen in beautiful Technicolor was a pornographic movie that the patient was watching when he started exhibiting the chest pain. Not able to contain herself, the EMS Captain started laughing, further hastening the embarrassed patient's quest for the remote. With the wife finally finding it, the peep show was turned off, and all went back to their assigned duties of tending to the patient. Now, every time Bobay drives by the house, she thinks about what was on the television that day, wondering when she'll be called back for another early morning show!

Robin S. Bobay, EMS Captain/FF. Northeast Allen County. Fire and EMS Inc. Grabill, Indiana

157

WHEN GOD MADE EMT'S

Some choices in life are easy. Others take some deep soul searching. Heather Wilhelm of Collinsville, Illinois, knew hers would be the latter. With a long medical history of her own, she wasn't sure if a career in the emergency medical field would be her calling. It wasn't until a friend, who was a veteran EMT-P, gave her some career advice and sent her the following story that she was able to make the decision that would change the course of her life: the choice to become an EMT.

WHEN GOD MADE EMT'S. When the Lord made EMT's, he was into his sixth day of overtime when an angel appeared and said, "You're doing a lot of fiddling around on this one." And the Lord said, "Have you read the specs on this order? An EMT has to be able to carry an injured person up a wet, grassy hill in the dark, dodge stray bullets to reach a dying child unarmed, enter homes the health inspector wouldn't touch and not wrinkle his uniform. He has to be able to lift 3 times his own weight, crawl into wrecked cars with barely enough room to move and console a grieving mother as he does CPR on a baby he knows will never breath again. He has to be in top mental condition at all times, running on no sleep, black coffee and half-eaten meals. And he needs to have six pairs of hands." The angel shook her head slowly and said, "Six pairs of hands...no way." "It's not the hands that are causing me problems," said the Lord, "It's the three pairs of eyes a medic needs to have." "That's on the standard model?" asked the angel. The Lord nodded. "One pair that sees open sores as he is drawing blood and asks the patient if they may be HIV positive, (when he already knows and wishes he had taken that accounting job). Another in the side of the head for his partner's safety. And yet another pair of eyes in front that can look reassuringly at a bleeding victim and say, "You'll be all right ma'am," when he knows it isn't so." "Lord," said the angel, touching his sleeve, "rest and work on this tomorrow." "I can't," said the Lord,

"I already have a model that can talk a 250-pound drunk out from behind a steering wheel without incident and feed a family of five on a private service paycheck." The angel circled the model of the EMT very slowly, "Can it think?" she asked. "You bet," said the Lord. "It can tell you the symptoms of 100 illnesses; recite drug calculations in its sleep; intubate, defibrillate, medicate and continue CPR nonstop over terrain that any doctor would fear...and still it keeps its sense of humor. This medic also has phenomenal personal control. He can deal with a multi-victim trauma, coax a frightened elderly person to unlock their door, comfort a murder victim's family and then read in the daily paper how EMT's were unable to locate a house quickly enough, allowing the person to die. A house which had no street signs, no house numbers, no phone to call back." Finally, the angel bent over and ran her finger across the cheek of the EMT. "There's a leak," she pronounced. "I told you that you were trying to put too much into this model." "That's not a leak," said the Lord, "It's a tear." "What's the tear for?" asked the angel. "It's for bottled-up emotions, for patients they've tried in vain to save. For commitment to that hope that they will make a difference in a person's chance to survive—For life." "You're a genius," said the angel. The Lord looked somber. "I didn't put it there," he said.

-Author Unknown

Heather Wilhelm, EMT. Laughlin Ambulance Service. Troy, Illinois.

THEY CALL ME MR. TWINKLE TOES

In the world of ski patrol, the first thing to remember is what goes up must come down. In the case of EMT Matt S., sometimes things go up, down, up, down, up. While practicing evacuation techniques in the event of a broken down chairlift, Patroller Matt S. was in charge of the belay line that was attached to a chairlift some thirty feet above his head. It was Matt's responsibility to keep tension on the line while his fellow patroller, acting as a trapped victim in the chair above, strapped himself onto a t-shaped seat attached to the same rope. New to the technique, Matt had inadvertently stepped out of a stable position. With Matt only weighing about 160-pounds and the mock victim tipping the scale at over 200, the laws of physics quickly took hold. Holding the rope with dogged determination as the weight came on, Matt suddenly found himself being pulled across the snow as his partner above dropped towards the ground. As the rope system came into equilibrium, Matt bounced up into the air and down again like a yo-yo, looking more like a ballerina than a ski patroller. Following procedure, another team member was standing nearby, ready to assist. Witnessing the dance in the snow, the other member quickly took hold of Matt, adding the needed counterweight and allowing Matt to resume lowering the passenger safely to the ground. It wasn't too long after the incident that Matt was dubbed with his new nickname. So if you're ever skiing in New Hampshire and are in need of a rescuer, just ask for Mr. Twinkle Toes.

Matt S., OEC, EMT-Intermediate. New Hampshire.

SHARK ATTACK

Lifeguard Crystal Lavinder has worked in Myrtle Beach, South Carolina, most of her career. In addition to her regular lifeguard duties, she is also an instructor and specializes in teaching the pier rescue portion of the Horry County Rookie Lifeguard School. The object of the session is to teach the new lifeguards how to rescue victims under a pier that might get caught in a rip current or possibly become the casualty of a wave that could send them crashing into a piling. If that training isn't difficult enough, the area around the pier is also known to be a hunting ground for large sharks. During one such training session everything was proceeding well for Lavinder, her partner instructor, and the group of students. When the students started getting arm fatigued, Lavinder suggested that they put their legs down to tread, resting the arms. Feeling arm fatigued herself, Lavinder took her own advice dropping her legs down to tread. When she did this, she kicked what felt like a dorsal fin to her. Her partner quickly sensed a look of fear on her face and asked what was wrong. Lavinder replied, "Dude, I think I just kicked a dorsal—no, I *know* I just kicked a dorsal fin of a shark!" Unfortunately, she said it loud enough for the group of students to hear. All of them stopped dead in the water, eyes as big as saucers. They quickly looked at each other, then turned and started swimming as fast as they could to the safety of shore. Wanting to have some fun, Lavinder's partner picked up a harmless, non-stinging cannon ball jellyfish swimming nearby and threw it at the students. The jellyfish projectile hit one of the students on the shoulder, causing him to scream, which in turn caused the instructors to laugh. After a quick discussion, the instructors figured the shark's dorsal fin that Lavinder felt was probably just a jellyfish. Just in case, though, they finished that day's training set pretty quick!

Crystal Lavinder, Lifeguard, Myrtle Beach, South Carolina

HARD TO SWALLOW

Nothing pulls more at the heart strings of a first responder than a young child in distress. One day Firefighter Leo Byrne, of the Los Angeles City Fire Department, responded to such a call, receiving a response for a three-year-old male in respiratory distress. Working on a BLS ambulance at the time, Leo and his partner arrived on scene being told the patient was on the couch in the living room. Quickly moving to render aid, the two firefighters got to the room, only to discover a fifty-year-old male and an approximately three-year-old dog sitting on the couch. You guessed it, they had been called for the dog that had apparently swallowed a chicken bone and began choking. After taking a quick assessment, including lung sounds (at least Byrne thought he was listening to the lungs), they quickly cancelled the paramedic ambulance that was responding with them and informed the owners that the dog seemed fine, but he would still need to be checked out by a vet!

Leo Byrne, Firefighter. Los Angeles City Fire Department. California

JUST THE FACTS

Skunked again? This time forget the tomato juice. If your animal has a run in with a skunk, try a mixture of 10 parts hydrogen peroxide to 1 part baking soda. Add a dash of degreasing dishwashing soap and pour into a spray bottle. Spray liberally over dry coat and allow to air dry. Avoid eyes. Works on inanimate objects too!

SAFETY BULLETIN

Heimlich maneuver for cats and dogs: After determining that your pet is choking, remove any item that may be constricting the neck. Examine inside the mouth and remove any foreign object you see. Do not blindly place your hand down your pet's throat and pull any object you feel. Dogs have small bones that support the base of their tongues. Owners probing the throat for a foreign object have mistaken these for chicken bones. Do not attempt to remove an object unless you can see and identify it. If your pet is small and you cannot easily remove the object, lift and suspend him with the head pointed down. For larger animals, lift the rear legs so the head is tilted down. This can help dislodge an item stuck in the throat. Another method is to administer a sharp blow with the palm of your hand between the shoulder blades. This can sometimes dislodge an object. If this does not work, a modified Heimlich maneuver can be attempted.

- Grasp the animal around the waist so that the rear is nearest to you, similar to a bear hug.
- Place a fist just behind the ribs.
- Compress the abdomen several times (usually 3-5 times) with quick pushes.
- Check the mouth to see if the foreign object has been removed.
- This maneuver can be repeated one to two times but if not successful on the first attempt, make arrangements to immediately take your pet to the nearest veterinary hospital.

Even if you are successful in removing a foreign object, veterinary examination is recommended. Internal injury could have occurred that you may not realize. If you follow only these instructions, you do so at your own risk since this page has not been approved by a DVM.

Captain David Griffith of the Durham Fire Department, North Carolina has had a long and successful career as a fire officer. Throughout his career he has documented the funny and unusual on-duty events he has encountered by means of skillfully illustrating cartoons. The following cartoon is an example of his work.

Have you been spanking the monkey?

A call came in the wee hours of the morning at Station #5 in reference to a baby having respiratory distress. The crew arrived to find the residence full of free roaming animals, and a man and woman holding an apparently unconscious baby monkey. The couple was afraid if they told 911 that the baby was a baby monkey, the response would not have been expedient. The baby monkey was revived.

WORD FOR WORD

The English language is filled with words that sound the same, but have different meanings, which are called homonyms. Sometimes these words can cause confusion for some first responders, especially rookies responding to their first motor vehicle accident (MVA). Arriving at the scene of a MVA in a rural part of West Virginia, EMT-B Donna Steward of the Springfield Area Rescue Squad made her way to one of the cars with the aid of a firefighter carrying her across a field of brush, briars, and stickers. Steward quickly instructed the firefighter to hold traction on the patient's neck just in case of a spinal injury. She then called out to her partner, who was new to the emergency service, that she needed him to get her a 4x4 for the patient. Thinking he knew what she needed, the rookie EMT ran over to the fire chief of the Springfield Valley Volunteer Fire Department and asked him for a 4x4 piece of wood. The chief, who just happened to be Steward's nephew, and an EMT-B himself, asked the rookie what he needed the wood for. The rookie insistently replied that Steward needed the piece of wood to stabilize the patient's neck. Questioning the rookie's unusual request, the chief called out to his aunt asking her why she needed a 4x4 piece of wood. Laughing aloud, Steward quickly replied that she needed a 4x4 piece of gauze, not wood, to cover a small cut on the patient's forehead. Later that year, the fire department held its annual banquet. There, the homonymous challenged rookie was presented with an award of such. You guessed it—a 4x4 piece of wood with a 4x4 piece of gauze taped to it.

Donna Steward, EMT-B. Springfield Area Rescue Squad, Inc. West Virginia.

FINDING THE HUMOR IN THINGS

First responders are not super heroes. They are just ordinary human beings asked to sometimes do extraordinary things. Requested daily to deal with a multitude of different situations, they must often suppress their emotions in order to deal with the stress involved. Some of the situations are sad, others even sadder, and after the emergency is resolved, first responders are often in need of stress release. Though some time must elapse before one can see the humor in a situation, finding that humor is essential for adequate stress release. Often using this method, firefighter/paramedics with the King George County Emergency Services were dispatched to a suicidal subject. Upon arrival, they found a 17-year-old male with multiple contusions and abrasions about his face and head. The paramedics began assessing the patient and questioning him as to the cause of his injuries. The patient stated that in a desperate attempt to end his life, he had put one of his mother's nitroglycerin pills in his mouth and proceeded to slam his head into inanimate objects with the hope of causing the nitroglycerin to explode! After helping the boy get through the ordeal, the first responders returned to the station chuckling among themselves about the serious, but humorous encounter.

Shawn M. McDermott, FF/PM. King George County Emergency Services. Virginia

166

FREQUENT FLYER

Frequent Flyers. We have all heard the term used. Most think it only applies to someone that travels a lot by air, such as a businessperson or a sales rep. In the first responder community, however, the term is used to describe an individual that frequently calls 911 for help. One night while Kami Welch was doing "ride time" to become an EMT-B, she and her two paramedic partners received a dispatch call. The paramedics immediately recognized the address as that of a frequent flyer's house. Arriving on scene, Kami and the paramedics found the familiar elderly resident inside, praying with her daughter, and telling her that she would see her in heaven. Hearing this, Kami and the paramedics went to work, taking vitals and starting an I.V. As they did so, they repeatedly heard the older woman say she needed a *"vibrator."* Trying to be as professional as possible, Kami and the paramedics did their best not to laugh, quickly transporting the woman to the hospital. Along the way, the patient again repeated her odd request for a *"vibrator."* It was not until they arrived at the hospital that they figured out that the woman was not asking for a *vibrator*, but, instead a *ventilator!*

Kami Welch, EMS Director. Lucas First Responders, Iowa

IT'S ALL IN THE DELIVERY

Since the beginning of time, women have given birth to children with little or no medical assistance from the outside world. However, with the advances in modern medicine, along with the development of the 911 system, the community at large has become dependent on medical intervention. The following story is a prime example of how true this statement really is. During a particularly busy 24-hour shift in Hot Springs, Arkansas, James Stine, a paramedic with Lifemobile EMS, responded to a report of a woman giving birth. While enroute to the call, Stine received an update, via the radio, that the baby had self-delivered and was doing fine. Closing in on the reported address, Stine was met by an escort in the form of a very excited man driving a pick-up truck, and a young girl passenger who waived at them to follow them to another location.

Off the pick-up went, spilling dirt from its tires as it sped down the dusty road, finally coming to an abrupt stop some half mile from the original reported location. Stine watched as the female passenger exited the truck in a panic and ran up to him, grabbing him by the arm and signaling him to follow her. As he did, a bystander informed him that the young girl was deaf; however, she did read lips. Arriving at an abandoned car, Stine looked on with a tightening stomach as the 16-year-old girl reached inside and turned around with her hands outstretched. Expecting to see a newborn human baby cradled in her hands, Stine was surprised to see a newborn kitten instead. Not knowing exactly how to react to the feline findings, the stunned paramedic turned to his partner with his mouth wide open in astonishment. Being the professional he was, though, he soon gathered his composure and returned his attention back to the girl and the delivering mother. In all, six kittens were born. It turns out that the miscommunication of the birth was the result of the excited deaf girl running to a neighbor's house to report the birth, who in turn misunderstood her, thinking that a human being

needed medical assistance. Checking that there were no pregnant humans at the residence, Stine concluded the call by humorously reporting to his dispatch center that they were now "in service with six kittens, with no patient contact."

James Stine, Paramedic. Lifemobile EMS, Arkansas

JUST THE FACTS

Famous singer Johnny Cash was born in Kingsland, Arkansas.

PURPLE POD

Working as a medical response technician, Frank Silye Jr, has had the opportunity to meet many colorful people. At the beginning his career, he was doing a ride-a-long with the Cromwell Fire Department, observing fire department medics as they responded to a call at a nursing home for an emergency committal. It was reported that a woman was being aggressive and fighting with the staff and other patients. On the way, the medics discussed that it would probably be a quick "throw'em on the stretcher and go" type of call with the patient being described as a 90-year old woman. Walking up to the front desk, they asked the nurse on duty that night where the patient was. The nurse replied that they had just passed by her as they entered. Turning around, they saw an elderly woman sitting in the corner, quietly reading a magazine to herself. They had noticed her earlier; however, they hadn't paid much attention to her due to her calm demeanor. Slowly approaching the docile-looking woman, the medics began speaking to her, only to get silence for their response. The woman just sat there, reading aloud the same line over and over from the magazine she was holding. Eventually, the EMS lieutenant who was riding with Silye caught her attention and she began to tell her story to him. Trying to be polite, everyone listen attentively for a few moments. Ultimately hearing enough, the medics then asked the lady to sit on their stretcher for a ride over to the hospital. The once passive woman suddenly became very loud and belligerent, refusing to go. Seeing they had no other choice, Silye and the rest of the first responders on scene grabbed her and placed her on the stretcher, all the while she continued to read her magazine. Eventually getting her to the hospital, the medics were directed to take her to the mental health observation room, better known as the "Purple Pod." Meeting the ever so cautious hospital staff at the pod, they helped transfer the patient into a bed. As they did, the woman began to talk about the contents of the article she was reading, referring to a section about "strippers."

Not paying much attention to her, Silye and his team began to leave the room. All of a sudden, the elderly woman turned to them and asked in a loud voice, "Are you going to strip for me tonight?" She then turned back to her magazine, leaving Silye stunned and the remaining members laughing hysterically. Back at the station, Silye had to endure additional questioning and teasing as to which colorful career he would now make his calling.

Frank Silye Jr, Medical Response Technician. Cromwell, Connecticut.

JOKE

The nurse said to the doctor, *"There's an invisible man in the waiting room."* The doctor replied, *"Tell him I can't see him now."*

REACTION

A Poem

I was working at a motocross
To deal with injuries.
Like bruised ribs and broken ankles,
Lacerations, and sprained knees.

Events designed for every age
And different size of bike,
Allowed small kids to be involved
If they would really like.

One young boy on fifty C's
was only five or four.
He missed a mogul on a jump
And landed pretty poor.

I hurried over to the scene
Because of his bad trip.
But when I checked him out I found
He'd only hurt his lip.

About that time the dad showed up
To check up on his boy.
The way he jerked that kid around
Was like some cheap, old toy.

He pushed me back out of his way
And with a verbal curse,
He made it known the boy would ride
Or he might get hurt worse.

He sat his son back on the bike
And with the kid in tears,
Sent boy and bike in route again
With no regard for fears.

I turned around and walked away.
This guy had changed my mood.
Now in my mind I did debate
His style of parenthood.

As I returned back to my post
And sat down on the dirt.
I squelched the urge to show that dad
How bad a lip can hurt.

Darryl Claassen, Chief. Whitewater River Fire District, Whitewater,
Kansas

LOST IN TRANSLATION

Every first responder knows that being teamed with a partner that has a good sense of humor will provide comic relief to a long stressful shift. Ian, a paramedic in London, England, was lucky to be teamed with such a funny and professional veteran medic. Ian was just beginning his EMS career and, as a trainee, he got crewed with the veteran for a couple of shifts. One particular rescue they handled was in an area near the station that had its fair share of drunks. Upon contact with the patient, it was fairly easy to tell the man had a little too much to drink. For the man's safety, the medics decided to take him to the local accident and emergency department to sober up. While driving the patient, Ian could hear his partner talking to the man in the back of the ambulance. What struck Ian as odd was his partner was speaking German when the patient was definitely a British man. At the next stop light Ian leaned back and asked his partner what he was doing. The medic replied, "Entertaining myself," and then turned back to the confused patient and said in his best German, "Was ist ihr name? (What is your name?) Sind sie wie alt? (How old are you?) Was ist ihr geburtsdatum? (What is your date of birth?)" and the remaining standard EMS questions. Hearing this foreign language, the patient just scratched his head and mumbled to himself as he stared out the window. At the hospital, the medics gave the hand over to the triage nurse, while the entire time the veteran spoke German to the un-amused staff. The drunken patient just sat in a chair with his head buried his hands, mumbling to himself quietly, "Am I in Germany? What the @!&* am I doing in Germany?" Looking up in despair at a nurse he then asked her, "Am I really in Germany?" The nurse folded her arms, looked him straight in the eye, and in her best German comedic accent said, "Are you in Germany? Yharrrr!" At that point the staff and the two medics burstout laughing. Once the patient sobered up a little, he too saw the funny side of it and was highly amused.

Ian, Paramedic. London, England

OH, LORDIE!

Throughout the world, people attend church to hear the word of God, taking the promise of everlasting life to heart. Some, however, take the word of the gospel too literally, setting in motion a chain of events such as in the following story. On one Sunday morning, EMT Cheryl Lassiter responded to a call of a female having a panic attack at a place of worship. Entering the church, Lassiter found the emotionally distressed patient sitting in a pew, repeatedly muttering the words, "Oooohh, Lordie; save me, Jesus!" Next to the anguished woman stood her daughter explaining to Lassiter that her mother was upset due to a religious misunderstanding. She relayed that "Momma" had misunderstood the preacher, thinking that he had said she was going to hell; however, he did not mean her personally. Eventually gathering all the facts, and completing a full examination of the woman, EMT Lassiter came to the diagnosis that the patient was suffering from either a case of "Tacha-Lordia" or "Juctional-Jesus," and that a higher source of help was in order.

Cheryl Lassiter, EMT-P / Firefighter. Texas

In Texas, "Y'all" can be used singular or plural.

WHO LET THE CATS OUT?

After graduating from basic training, first responders are sent off into the field to work. This is only the beginning, though, with many more important lessons to be learned, which we call experience. An experience to remember would be the lesson of the day for the rookie partner of veteran EMT John Sands. With the rookie fresh out of training school, their EMS unit was dispatched on a medical run to transport a mental patient in the city of Vandalia, Ohio. This particular address was well known by Sands to be the residence of a "frequent flyer," which is someone who routinely calls 911. The encounter with the mental patient was the first for the new medic who didn't key in on the word "mental." As the EMS crew pulled up to the house, Sands told the rookie to watch the front door and to be careful not to let any of the cats out of the house. Being new and wanting to do his best, the rookie diligently watched for any cats near the front door as he opened it just wide enough to squeeze in. While attending to the patient, Sands commented several times to his junior partner to watch out for the cats and to make sure not to step on them or let them get out. Based on the rookie's body language, Sands could tell he was watching closely for any cats. During the transport of the patient, the rookie leaned over to Sands and whispered that he didn't see any cats at the house. Just then, the patient seated on the cot in the back started waving at the back doors of the medic unit as she said, "Look at the nice kitty at the back window." With the medic unit traveling down the interstate at 60 miles per hour, and only one person seeing a cat, and it wasn't one of the EMS crew, the rookie finally got it! That day, the rookie learned two valuable lessons: one, take EMT veterans like Sands a little less seriously; and two, listen better to the description of the call. The "invisible cats" experience was one lesson the rookie carried with him throughout his successful career with the fire division.

John Sands, Retired Fire Chief. Presently with the Ohio Department of Public Safety as the EMS Education Coordinator.

INFORMATION BULLETIN

The **"Star of Life"** is a six barred blue cross representing the six critical elements of Emergency Medical Services (EMS) which are honored and trusted to optimize:

- Detection
- Reporting
- Response
- On-Scene Care
- Care in Transit
- Transfer to Definitive Care

THE POWER OF THE CROSS

The year 2005 will most likely be remembered as the year of Hurricane Katrina. One of the most devastating hurricanes to ever hit the Gulf Coast of the United States, it brought with it death and destruction on biblical proportions. Though there were many horrific scenes of tragedy, Jason Zigmont, a firefighter/paramedic working with AMR Ambulance Services, was witness to at least one miracle. While assigned to the rescue/relief effort in Mississippi, Zigmont came upon St. Paul's Catholic Church, located in the town of Pass Christian. The church was originally built to withstand a category five hurricane. With its white steeple roof, along with its beautiful stain glass frontage, it was a monument to man's ingenuity and design. Unfortunately, that was before Katrina. After the hurricane, all that remained was a torn out shell and a tangled mess of pews. Not all was lost, though, as God works in mysterious ways. Looking around, Zigmont viewed what could only be described as Devine intervention. Hanging on the Sanctuary wall, unscathed from all the destruction was a large crucifix. As if that wasn't proof enough of God's will, the stained glass "Stations of the Cross" that stood in the front of the building was completely intact. Even with all of the destruction around it, the glass itself didn't display so much as a chip of imperfection. When it comes to such wonders, Zigmont thought a local paramedic summed it up best, saying, "I'm not religious, but that could make a believer out of me." Hopefully, more people will see it that way, too!

Jason Zigmont. Firefighter/Paramedic. East Berlin Volunteer Fire Company Inc., Connecticut. First-Hand Account from Hurricane Katrina Rescue/Relief Effort, Mississippi. **www.VolunteerFD.org** - Owned and operated by Jason Zigmont. This online organization is dedicated to bringing volunteers together to share information on bylaws, grants, SOGs, recruitment and retention, and fundraising.

178

WILL THE REAL PATIENT PLEASE STAND UP!

As a first responder, you must sometimes act fast and make split-second decisions. Unfortunately, this quick action can sometimes lead to jumping to conclusions. This next tale of tribulation comes from Tim Maltas, an EMT from the state of Illinois. The story starts with Tim receiving a call from a woman who was four-months pregnant and complaining of vaginal bleeding. Pulling up to the reported address, which was located in a mostly Hispanic neighborhood, Tim and his partner noticed a group of women standing at the curb, along with a middle-aged woman, waving at them from the doorway of a home. Assuming the patient was inside the house, Tim's partner immediately grabbed the jump bag and headed inside, while Tim retrieved the cot. As he did so, three young Hispanic women at the curb climbed in the open side door of the ambulance, one stating in broken English, "We go to the hospital." Trying to explain to them that the ambulance was not for the entire family, Tim asked them to please get out; however, they didn't move. Again, Tim asked them to leave, this time more forcefully, telling them to, "Get out!" The women immediately complied, giving Tim an offensive look as they exited. As Tim was closing the doors to the ambulance, his partner came running back out of the house with new information that one of the three women just happened to be the patient. Embarrassed, Tim then had to convince the woman to get back into the ambulance, which she did reluctantly, and with a slight attitude. In the future, Tim has promised to have a little more patience when it comes to patients

Tim Maltas, EMT-I. Peru Volunteer Ambulance Service, Illinois

A Leg Up

In the field of EMS, paramedics and EMT's alike are exposed to a number of agonizing sights. Thankfully, though, some of the patients look a lot worse on first glance than they really are. This is especially true with the following story. An Orange City ambulance crew was dispatched to a call of an elderly woman who had fallen down some stairs. Upon arrival, the patient was found silently lying at the bottom of a dark staircase. From first glance, the EMT's noticed that one of the woman's legs was severely angulated, bending backwards in an unnatural position! Horrified at the sight, the EMT grimaced in sympathetic pain for the patient. He would not suffer long, though. Luckily, the other EMT on scene was familiar with the patient. With a smile on his face, the second EMT bent down, picked up the patient's leg, and handed it to his partner—it was a prosthesis. This only goes to prove that a good partner is always there to give you a *LEG UP* when you need one.

Brian Paugh, Paramedic, Iowa

Do Roman paramedics refer to IV's as 4's?

LONDON CALLING

Stress knows no boundaries, nor does it care what country you live in. The following story comes all the way from London, England, where paramedics of the London Ambulance Service received a radio call to a reported stabbing. The transmission had come in very scratchy and lacked specifics. Wanting additional information, one of the medics quickly asked the dispatch center where the patient was stabbed. Expecting an answer such as "in the chest or stomach," the dispatch center simply replied, "in the west end." Not sure what to expect when they arrived on the scene, the same curious medic found a group of French tourists anxiously standing outside the reported address. He quickly asked one of them if he knew where the victim was stabbed. The person answered, "in the phone booth." It was now clear to the first responder that he wouldn't receive the answer he was looking for. Eventually though, they found the patient who had thankfully received only a minor laceration to the right hand and was not stabbed "in the phone booth" or "in the west end."

Name withheld per request. London, England

JUST THE FACTS

Scratching makes an itch worse because it releases histamine from mast cells, which stimulates the itch. Apply an ice pack, a cold water compress or an antihistamine.

Captain David Griffith of the Durham Fire Department, North Carolina has had a long and successful career as a fire officer. Throughout his career he has documented the funny and unusual on-duty events he has encountered by means of skillfully illustrating cartoons. The following cartoon is an example of his work.

Do you have any history of hypertension, diabetes, heart problems, termites, carpenter ants....?

Firefighters from Fire Station #2 responded to a patient possibly having a stroke. They arrived to find the elderly gentleman in relatively good shape except for a little disorientation. Sensory and motor functions were assessed in all extremities, and the patient's right leg seemed a little weak. The firefighter asked if that was normal for his right leg, and the gentleman revealed that he had a prosthesis.

PRIORITY LESSON

The following tale is a prime example that we all need to get our priorities straight in life. It was Halloween night when Vickie Brown, an EMT-B with the Woodburn First Responders was called out to a motor vehicle accident on a dirt road just south of her small country town of Woodburn, Iowa. When she arrived on scene, the driver of the car was standing in the middle of the road, walking around and screaming something about a "cow." Wanting to start treatment, Brown convinced the man to sit down. With the first responders asking him what had happened, the driver replied that he had hit a cow on the way to a Halloween party and that he was worried that he had really hurt it. Knowing the cow's fate, they broke the news gently to the man that the cow would have to be put down. Concerned with the patient's well-being, Brown and her fellow first responders then took c-spine precautions, securing the man to a backboard. It was not until sometime later when they were loading the man into the ambulance, the man finally asked, "How's my wife and daughter?" Brown, thinking "Go figure, the cow was his first priority," was surprised at how long it took the man to shift his thoughts from the injured cow to his family. Trying to control her anger, she replied that his family was fine and was already at the county hospital. As they began their transport of the patient, the man continued to talk about the cow, occasionally complaining about how tight he was immobilized and asking the EMT's if they had used duct tape. Thinking the man was in need of a lesson in priorities, thoughts of securing him further, this time with "duct tape," flashed through Brown's mind. To this day, Brown and her crew laugh about this call, carrying a role of duct tape on board as a joke and as a reminder of the real priorities in life.

Vickie Brown, EMT-B. Woodburn First Responders. Iowa

183

LIFE'S A BEACH

So you want to be a lifeguard. Beach, sand, sun, bikinis, oh and let's not forget tornados. That's right, TORNADOS! Myrtle Beach Lifeguard Philip Cotton will tell you that life is not always just a beach in South Carolina. In the summer of 2001, while packing up his lifeguard tower to close out another day of sunburns and near drownings, Lifeguard Cotton noticed the weather conditions quickly changing. With sand blowing hard in his face, Cotton turned to look at the local pier just in time to see a large lightning bolt strike it. He next witnessed approximately 50 or so people scrambling off the wooden structure for safety. Suddenly, as if God opened up the sky and exhaled, the sand dunes went flat, showing not a blemish in their mist. From behind him, Cotton next felt a tap on his shoulder. He turned to find a concerned woman warning him of the large funnel cloud hurling towards them, a mere 800 meters away. Quickly reporting the situation to his dispatch center, Cotton proceeded to run off the beach to safety, warning all he came in contact with to seek shelter. Hearing this, another woman stopped him, and with a strong southern accent, said, "Son, we don't have tornados here. This isn't Kansas, Dear." Since he was originally from the United Kingdom and new to the area, Cotton didn't argue with her. Instead, he ignored her insistence, pivoting her around to give her full view of the tornado that Myrtle Beach supposedly didn't have. Seeing the thunderous vortex, the woman began screaming wildly in fear, "There's a tornado on the beach. Run for your lives!" Hearing this, Cotton then replied in a sarcastic voice, "That's what I've been trying to tell you!" Eventually making it safely to a nearby hotel, he met up with two other lifeguards that he worked with, along with approximately 40 civilians. This is where he heard his next bizarre statement. "Thank goodness you guys are here," a man called out from the crowd. Cotton returned his praise with an exasperated look and replied in an authoritative voice, "Sir, I'll save you if you're drowning; however,

even this one is out of my control." With everyone now huddled on the floor, the wind intensified, attempting to pull all from within outside. Women and children began screaming and crying, men were shaking in fear, and Cotton began saying a prayer to the Man upstairs. The tornado eventually passed and all were safe. Cotton and his fellow survivors then went outside to survey the damage. Debris covered the beach for as far as the eye could see. Police, fire, and rescue personnel were now patrolling the area. Cotton stopped one of the first responders and asked him, "Who's going to clean up all this mess?" Chuckling, the officer answered, "Well, under the city's contract with the beach lifeguard service, it's the lifeguard's duty to maintain a clean and safe beach environment." During his career, Cotton had often heard that he had the best job in the world, however, not that summer.

Philip Cotton, Lifeguard. Myrtle Beach, South Carolina

JUST THE FACTS

The first battle of the Civil War took place at Fort Sumter located in South Carolina.

FORCED ENTRY

Larry Rand is currently working as a New York/New Jersey police officer for the Port Authority at La Guardia Airport. Back in the early 1980's, however, he was working as a paramedic for NYC* EMS. One hot summer day in July, 1984, he and his female partner got a call for a woman down in an apartment in Bedford Styvestant, located in the city of Brooklyn, New York. Since the dispatch was an unknown medical type call, they treated it as a cardiac response. Arriving at the apartment in well under five minutes, the medics rang the doorbell and heard a female voice inside plead, "Help me...PLEASE." Quickly, Rand tried the door handle, but it was locked. He then tried to force open the door, but it proved too strong an opponent for the 5'4", 185-pound medic. Rand then called for backup from the NYPD but found that there were no police officers available at the time to assist. Next, he put in a call to the nearest fire company, but they were also busy on a call and the relocating unit was still 10-15 minutes out. Yelling through the closed door, Rand told the victim to stay calm and that help was on the way. The woman replied back, "I'm having another heart attack...please get in here." The medics knew that if they decided to wait the 10-15 minutes for backup, the victim might die. They also knew that if they took the time to enter the victim's fifth floor apartment by way of the fire escape, the victim might also die. Figuring the best way to get to the victim would be to try again to force entry on the front door, Rand kicked and kicked the door, and then with one more huge kick, he was able to get the door to move a little. Seeing some progress from his assault, he stepped back and with all the might he could muster, he kicked again and finally the door crashed open. The medics promptly started the workup on the patient, who was obviously having some sort of cardiac episode. As Rand knelt next to the patient to start treatment, she looked up at him and as plain as day said, "It was a pull door!" In the end,

everything turned out fine; the patient recovered nicely at the hospital and was released two weeks later. About a week later, though, the same two medics were asked by a local councilman to make a courtesy visit to the patient's apartment. Upon arriving, they found the fully recovered patient standing outside her apartment unit holding a sheet over the door and smiling. The woman then removed the sheet to reveal to the medics a newly installed door, compliments of the city. Unlike the other door, however, this one came with instructions. The woman had humorously placed a large "X" on the door marking the spot where the paramedic had kicked and also a small sign next to it that said, "PULL." Everyone had a good laugh.

Larry Rand, Port Authority Police Officer. La Guardia Airport, New York

"We will never forget the Heroes of 9/11....37 PAPD, 343 FDNY, 23 NYPD, 3 NYSC and dozens more."

JUST THE FACTS

HOUSE NUMBERS—Be sure your house number is visible from the road. Put the numbers on your mailbox or a post near your driveway. Use numbers that are at least three inches tall. Think about using the reflecting type!

187

WHAT A TURD!

Ask any EMT or paramedic and they'll tell you that they never know what to expect when they get called to an emergency. Sometimes it is as simple as putting a band-aid on a minor cut, while other times it's just pure...well, let the following story explain. Responding to an unknown type medical call, Kanawha County Emergency Ambulance Authority Paramedics arrived on scene and were greeted by an elderly woman explaining that her husband was having abdominal pain. Trying to get a complete medical history of her husband, the medics started asking her questions. Instead of answering the questions, the woman simply handed them a plastic lunch bag containing a 6 inch log of human feces, the woman stating, "I thought you might need a stool sample."

Greg Wolfe, Paramedic. Kanawha County Emergency Ambulance Authority. Charleston, West Virginia

SAFETY BULLETIN

ICE: In Case of Emergency
Paramedics will often turn to a victim's cell phone for clues to that person's identity. You can make their job much easier with a simple idea that they are trying to get everyone to adopt: ICE, which stands for In Case of Emergency. If you add an entry in the contacts list in your cell phone under ICE, with the name and phone number of the person that the emergency services should call on your behalf, you can save them a lot of time and have your loved ones contacted quickly. It only takes a few moments of your time to do.

A MISUNDERSTANDING

Spanning the career of a first responder, there always seems to be at least one embarrassing episode that they wish could be magically erased from time. The following is one such anecdote that Blair Howe from the Milliken Fire Protection District, located in the state of Colorado, wished never happened. While participating in an EMT basic training scenario, Howe and his group were assigned a health problem involving a young female patient with an unknown medical crisis. Performing as complete of an evaluation on the patient as possible, Blair was still unclear as to her given problem. Observing that Howe was having difficultly, one of the instructors asked him, "What is her mentation?"(Referring to whether or not her thought process was okay.) Suddenly a light bulb went on in his head, and he replied, "Oh, yeah, good idea!" He then turned to the female patient and asked her, "When was your last menstrual period?"

Blair Howe, Division Chief. Milliken Fire Protection District, Colorado

WORDS OF WISDOM

"Experience is the name a wise person gives to his own mistakes."

189

PICK A PART

As a brand new rookie, Deb Banish, a FF1/EMT with the Wheatland Fire Department, thought she was ready to handle anything. Unfortunately, she would soon find out that the job of a first responder is full of unexpected surprises and that you never know what could be tossed your way. Responding to a motor vehicle accident (MVA) on Wyoming State Highway 125 Southbound, Banish arrived on scene to a car that had rolled off the road, landing on its side. With EMS and another fire truck (Unit 12) already on scene and helping a trapped victim, Banish stepped out of her truck (Unit 17) and grabbed some cribbing for stabilization of the crashed vehicle. As she did this, she heard a man screaming in the distance. She looked around to discover him lying some fifteen feet from the crash site, his body partially covered by some tall grass that lined the side of the road. "My leg, my leg!" she heard him repeat over and over. Thinking this could be the defining moment in her career that tested everything she had learned in training, Banish made her way over to the down man. As she did, someone off in the distance complied with the man's repeated request, tossing him his separated leg. The blood immediately drained from Banish's face as she looked on in shock. Her distress soon turned to embarrassment, though, as she quickly discovered the leg was not real, but instead a prosthesis.

Deb Banish, FF1/EMT—Wheatland Fire Department, Wyoming.

Rx Mix Up

Taking a medical history from a woman who had possibly broken her hip after falling from a horse, Captain Garrett de Jong of the McCall Fire Department asked the patient if she was on any medication, and if so, had she taken any that day. With her husband by her side, the distressed lady replied that she had taken three Viagra pills. "Viagra?" the surprised captain questioned. "Yes, Viagra!" the husband confirmed. Giving the couple a puzzling look, the captain started to note the given information in his medical report. Suddenly, the couple yelled out in unison, "Oh no, not Viagra....Allegra!"

Captain Garrett de Jong, McCall Fire Protection District. Idaho

JUST THE FACTS

Under Idaho law only two forms of city government are allowed: a mayor/councilor or a council/manager form.

FINDING THE HUMOR IN THINGS

First responders are not super heroes. They are just ordinary human beings asked to sometimes do extraordinary things. Requested daily to deal with a multitude of different situations, they must often suppress their emotions in order to deal with the stress involved. Some of the situations are sad, others even sadder, and after the emergency is resolved, first responders are often in need of stress release. Though, some time must elapse before one can see the humor in a situation, finding that humor is essential for adequate stress release. Often using this method, Firefighter/Paramedics with the King George County Emergency Services were dispatched to a suicidal subject. Upon arrival, they found a seventeen-year-old male with multiple contusions and abrasions about his face and head. The paramedics began assessing the patient and questioning him as to the cause of his injuries. The patient stated that in a desperate attempt to end his life, he had put one of his mother's nitroglycerin pills in his mouth and proceeded to slam his head into inanimate objects with the hope of causing the nitroglycerin to explode! Back at the station after helping the boy get through the ordeal, the first responders couldn't help but chuckle among themselves about the serious, but humorous encounter.

Shawn M. McDermott, FF/PM. King George County Emergency Services. Virginia

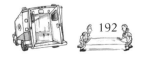

192

A FRIENDLY COMPETITION

Competition is alive and well in the "Friendship City" of Erlanger, Kentucky. For years, Captain Donna Sparks of Erlanger Fire/EMS and her best friend, who is a paramedic, had been trading practical jokes back and forth on each other, always looking for a way to outdo the other. One day while watching her mother-in-law repair some old furniture, Sparks had a vision of payback. Using the unused foam that her mother-in-law had discarded from reupholstering some chairs, Sparks acquired a nice spongy piece. Taking it to the kitchen and placing the foam in a nine inch cake pan, Sparks cut it to form the perfect desert. She next decorated the artificial cake with a layer of delicious white icing, topping it off with coconut and jelly beans. Sparks then had her brother, who was also a medic, deliver the fake cake to her best friend's fire house. Warning the crew of the practical joke, the trap was set. The next day, the victim came in to find the cake surrounded by plates and a pot of hot coffee. Told that the cake was a gift from a thankful nurse for a job well done, Spark's best friend picked up a knife and prepared to dig in. With all from the station in attendance, they watched as the unsuspecting medic tried to stick the knife into the cake, only to have it spring back at him. Though not in attendance, Sparks could hear his agony of defeat from across town, now knowing she was triumphantly the Queen of the Hill—at least for that moment!

Donna Sparks, Captain. Erlanger Fire/EMS. Erlanger, Kentucky

"To Our Town from the EMTs"

Author Unknown -

We're sorry if we wake you in the middle of the night,
But someone in your neighborhood is fighting for their life.

We're sorry if we block the road and make you turn around,
But there's been a bad wreck - people dying on the ground.

When you see us coming, we hope you understand,
Let us have the right of way, someone heeds a helping hand.

Sometimes a person is choking, sometimes a broken leg,
Sometimes a heart stops beating, when we get there, it's too late.

So if you see us crying, when we think we are alone,
You'll know we've had a "bad one", and we're feeling mighty down.

You ask us why we do it, "How can you watch them die?"
It's never very easy, but we'll try to tell you why.

Somewhere deep within us, our souls are crying out,
"We're here to help our neighbors in their hour of pain and doubt."

God gave us something special to help us see you through.
We do it 'cause we love you and we care about you too.

Poem submitted by Diane Saunders, a retired EMT of 12 years for Middleton EMS, Middleton, Wisconsin and now on a disaster medical assistance Team (MN-1 DMAT) This poem was handed out to everyone who attended the Annual Emergency Medical Service Banquet, given to recognize volunteers by the City of Middleton, Wisconsin, on February 19, 2000.

THE GOOD OL' DAYS

Back before there were fancy titles like EMT or Paramedic, Max Hayes, from the Bremerton Fire Department, did his job with a good old fashioned first aid card. While working on an engine company in the early 1960's, Firefighter Hayes responded to medical call. Arriving at a residence, he was directed by a woman to go to a back room. There he found a man sitting on the bed, bleeding profusely from the head with bloody towels and washcloths scattered all about. The man was obviously intoxicated with the smell of alcohol reeking from his pores. Turning towards the woman, Hayes asked her what had happened. She replied, "I hit the son-of-a-bitch in the head with a whiskey bottle!" With the cause of the injury determined, Hayes and his partner quickly went to work on the bloody patient. Taking some bandages, Hayes wrapped the man's head; however, the blood continued to flow. Finally, the hospital transport arrived and took over care of the patient. Since the good old days didn't offer the benefit of rubber gloves, Hayes went to the bathroom and began to wash the blood off his hands. Suddenly, Hayes heard laughter coming from the bedroom. Returning to see what was so funny, the personnel from the transporting unit told him that he had done a great job bandaging the guy's ear. There was only one problem—the wound was on top of his head.

Max Hayes, Firefighter. Bremerton Fire Department, Washington State.

DID YOU SAY TURN LEFT?

Even in this world of technological advances, where global positioning systems can direct you step by step to a specific location, first responders have to sometimes rely on "good ol' person-to- person communication to get to the scene of an emergency. While working as a volunteer dispatcher with the local county EMS and fire district, Donna Steward, an EMT-B in West Virginia, witnessed one new dispatcher's ability to adapt to a new and stressful call. With Air Care Helicopter, Trooper 5 responding from its Maryland base to a reported motor vehicle accident, the new dispatcher was supposed to look up the coordinates in the flip charts and relay the information to the pilot. Unfortunately, the dispatcher forgot the correct procedure, relying instead on good ol' fashion communication to direct the helicopter to the incident. When the pilot neared the area and asked for the needed coordinates, the dispatcher simply replied, "Follow Route 28 south to the stop light, turn left, go four miles to the Mountain Top Truck Stop, turn left, and then go approximately 5 miles and you'll see the fire trucks and ambulances on scene." Hearing the new dispatcher's effective, yet unusual method for giving coordinates to a helicopter, all in the dispatch center had a good laugh, realizing computers and satellites are great, but you can't go wrong with good ol' fashion know how!

Donna Steward—EMT-B. Springfield Area Rescue Squad, Inc. West Virginia.

WILD FLOWER

A stressful situation can be a life changing event. Whether it's at home, work, or even a war zone, one must be able to find "the wild flower in the field of weeds" in order to cope with the stress. Pat King, a contract Firefighter/EMT with the Department of Defense, stationed in Kabul, Afghanistan, in support of Operation Enduring Freedom, found his wild flower in the least likely of all places, the men's latrine. Just completing a long night of in-flight emergency calls, Firefighter/EMT Pat King entered the men's latrine located on Bagram Air Field. Glancing across the room, his eyes stumbled upon some freshly written graffiti littering the walls. The words read, "Jesus loves you, but everyone else thinks you're an asshole." After laughing at the graffiti quote, King thought about the saying for a while, causing him to shift his perception of life and work and allowing him to find his own "wild flower in the field of weeds." Soon after, this revelation caused him to return to church and begin a writing career, sharing his experiences with others. To the troops all over the world, we hope you find your wild flower, and thank you for protecting those in need.

Pat King, Firefighter/EMT. Bagram Fire Department. Kabul, Afghanistan

LEGEND OF THE TOILET MONSTER

We have all heard the urban legends about Big Foot, the Lock Ness Monster, and the Abominable Snowman. There is one folklore, however, that has been shaded in secrecy for hundreds of years, known only to a few select people that is, until now. We're talking about the dreaded Toilet Monster; that horrendous creature that seems to only appear between the hours of 2:00 to 5:00 a.m., mysteriously moving the toilet from beneath people everywhere. The following traumatic event will be burned in Captain Van Son's mind for the rest of his natural life. While working with Great Falls Fire Rescue he recaps for us one of his most horrendous encounters he's had with the creature. Climbing onboard Engine 1 in Great Falls, Montana, Van Son and his crew set off to a local nursing home for a reported lift assist call. Arriving on scene, they were met by a nurse reporting to them that one of their patients had fallen from the toilet and could not get up. Warning his crew of the possible dangers that awaited them, Van Son and his men carefully entered the building.

All of a sudden, the team of firefighters heard screams of help emanating from a bathroom. Listening carefully, the trained ears of Captain Van Son heard, "Hurry up, boys!" Cautiously making their way into the room, the rookie entered first. Unfortunately, he didn't heed the captain's early warnings to be careful, stepping directly into a large pile of poop. "One of the oldest tricks in the books played by the Toilet Monster," the captain thought. "I told him to be careful." Reassessing the situation, the team of firefighters came up with their next plan of action—to steer clear of any more piles of the dangerous poop. Assuring the woman was free of injuries, they asked her where she wanted to be placed. The woman replied, "On the pot, I have to finish my business! Oh, and while you're at it, can you grab me a clean night-gown?" Without thinking of their own safety, the firefighters quickly helped the patient up and placed her back onto the toilet while Captain

Van Son courageously volunteered to leave the bathroom to retrieve the clean nightgown. Returning, Captain Van Son handed the woman the clean nightgown, to which she replied, "Well, aren't you going to put it on me?" Not wanting to take all the glory, Van Son allowed his two firefighters to do the honors while he remained outside the room just in case the creature returned. With the woman all cleaned and dressed, the two firefighters then asked her where she would now like to be placed. The woman answered, "I still have to finish my business. Just get out for a few minutes." Fearing for the woman's well being, the men hesitantly complied, leaving the door cracked open so they could keep a close eye on her. With her mission accomplished, the three firefighters watched in horror as the woman wiped her bottom clean and then wiped her nose with the same folded piece of toilet paper. Turning toward his fellow firefighters, Captain Van Son asked in shocked astonishment, "Did you see that?" Trying not to respond with the primal emotional response of laughter caused by the unbelievably event, the two firefighters replied, "Yes!" All thoughts of laughter quickly diminished, though, when they heard the next dreaded voice of doom coming from the bathroom, "Okay, boys," the woman called out, "I'm ready to go back to bed!"

David Van Son, Captain. Great Falls Fire Rescue, Montana

199

GIVE ME THE FINGER

Just say No! A saying that Robin Bobay hopes her patient in the following story has taken to heart. On an emergency run for a reported vehicle rollover, Indiana Firefighter/Medic Bobay came across a young man who had just rolled his vehicle on a back country road. Resembling a bad copy of Garth, a character in the movie, "Wayne's World," the man sported the entire outfit, complete with the horn-rimmed glasses, long stringy blond hair, flannel shirt, and a pair of torn jeans. Picturing the character from the movie in her mind, Bobay couldn't help but laugh. Quickly wiping the smile from her face, Bobay went to work, doing a complete examination of the patient. As far as she could tell, the patient only showed signs of a broken finger. Before transporting the patient, Bobay was told by a police officer on scene that "Garth" had been smoking some pot earlier and then decided to drink a six pack of beer to come down from his high. With the ambulance on the way to the hospital, Bobay's colleague started to bandage the man's broken finger. Bobay quickly stopped her, telling her partner not to bother wrapping it because the E.R. was just going to take it off anyways. Hearing the medic's conversation, "Garth" started crying like a little baby with tears flowing. Bobay quickly asked him what the problem was. The man, misunderstanding the medic's dialogue, tearfully replied, "I don't want my finger taken off!"

Robin S. Bobay, EMS Captain/FF. Northeast Allen County Fire and EMS Inc. Grabill, Indiana

POLICE

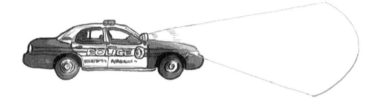

FIRST AMENDMENT

Don't believe everything you read in magazines. Deputy Leo Monahan of the Los Angeles County Sheriff's Department and his partner Deputy Steve Pair found this out the hard way while escorting a local reporter about town for a story he was doing on reserve deputies. Taking the journalist on a tour, the deputies showed him some hot locations for crime activity in their district. In casual conversation, the deputies told the reporter that in all their years in the area, they had never been shot at or had to shoot anyone. They did tell the reporter, however, that in the recent past, a man had discharged a shot gun into the air where they had been driving by. This particular incident caused every deputy from the West Hollywood Station to respond. A sergeant on scene eventually convinced the suspect to put the gun down and surrender. Not so long after the ride-a-long with the deputies ended, the reporter finished the article, and, as usual, the facts were all wrong. In the story, the reporter wrote that Deputy Monahan had been shot at 56 times in one particular alley in West Hollywood. Monahan paid the price for this misinformation, taking a severe ribbing from his peers. He also received a not so friendly call from the department's Information Bureau asking him, "What in hell had he told the reporter." All we can say is—blame it on the 1st Amendment!

Steve Pair, Reserve Deputy. Los Angeles County Sheriff's Department. California;
Appointed: February 1974 – **Retired:** January 1997
Leo Monahan, Reserve Deputy. Los Angeles County Sheriff's Department. California;
Appointed: May 6, 1973 – **Retired:** August 15, 1999 - In addition to his career in law enforcement, Monahan has also been very successful in the art world. He is the foremost paper sculpture illustrator in the country. He has taught art at Chouinard Art Institute, California Institute

of Art, Tokyo Communication Arts, Disney and USC. Monahan is also the designer of the Law Enforcement Memorial at the Los Angeles County Sheriff's "Star Center."

JUST THE FACTS

The "Flying Squad" came into existence in Los Angeles in 1918. It was equipped with two "high powered" automobiles operated by detectives after midnight to handle violent crimes commonly occurring during early morning hours. Violent crime obviously had no time clock. In the six-month period between October 1918 and March 1919, 17 police officers, two percent of all sworn personnel, lost their lives in the line of duty.

lacstores.co.la.ca.us/coroner—The Los Angeles County Coroner opened its Skeletons in the Closet souvenir shop in Los Angeles in 1993. Each souvenir-from beach towels to baseball caps-features a design, such as the L.A County seal, a chalk body outline or a skeleton dressed as Sherlock Holmes. Profits fund educational efforts about the conse-quences of drunk driving and drug abuse.

BEST IMPRESSIONS

A barricaded suspect is one of the most challenging of all police responses, requiring extra patience, along with a well thought out strategy. Sometimes though, all it takes to bring the incident to a satisfactory completion is a little ingenuity on the part of the officer(s) involved. Assigned as an assisting unit on a barricaded suspect call, Los Angeles County Deputy Sheriff Mike Ascolese took up position next to the deputy who was handling the incident. After exhausting all verbal attempts via his patrol car's PA system to get the suspect to give up and exit the house peacefully, the handling deputy came up with a fresh approach. The officer called out a warning to the barricaded man that a K-9 Unit had arrived on scene and would be deployed if the suspect didn't immediately exit the house peacefully. Knowing all too well that the K-9 and the Helicopter Units were no where near, and were unavailable for the assignment, Ascolese listened to his partner's instructions, wondering what he had up his sleeve. Receiving nothing but utter silence from the suspect, the comedic handling deputy then stated over the PA system that he was now letting the dog loose. Continuing to broadcast, he then did his best impression of a ferocious dog, barking loudly. As if by magic, the scared suspect instantaneously appeared outside the residence. Desperately darting his head around, searching for the non-existent K-9, the suspect was quickly taken into custody by a team of deputies. With the tense standoff concluded, the deputies all had a good laugh, benefiting from the entertaining impression.

Mike Ascolese, Deputy Sheriff. Los Angeles County Sheriff's Department, California

FATHER KNOWS BEST

Growing up in the Midwest with a dad who was a police officer for 27 years, Travis Yates wished he had a penny for every time he heard his dad say, "We don't catch the smart ones." It wasn't until Yates himself became a police officer for the Tulsa Police Department that he realized how right his dad had been. One summer evening, the younger Yates received a call of a rape that had occurred in a wooded area just outside an apartment complex. Hoping to make an arrest, Yates and his squad began the investigation. Familiar with this type of crime, Yates knew that, without physical evidence, a conviction was difficult to obtain and that the odds were against him making an arrest. Taking this into consideration, Yates and his team took the victim to the site where the rape had occurred in the hopes of finding something of value—and did they ever. Lying on top of a pile of leaves sat the most beautiful thing Yates had seen that night—a driver's license. Matching the description of the suspect with the license, Yates and his team quickly went to the suspect's home. There they found the suspect's wife who confirmed that her husband had just returned from the store, but had quickly left because his license had been lost. Yates thought, "You bet it was lost, and the Tulsa Police Department found it." Shortly after, the officers found out that the suspect was fleeing town. An officer contacted the suspect on his cell phone and was able to talk him into driving back home so he could be arrested. Although Yates' dad said, "We don't catch the smart ones," he never said anything about the dumb ones!

Travis Yates, Captain. Tulsa Police Department. Oklahoma

I DRIVE 55

Speed kills. We have all read the signs, but most still choose to ignore the message. Sergeant Michael Nihei of the Nevada Highway Patrol, knows that no matter what the posted speed limit, there will always be one person willing to push the envelope. The following story happened many years ago when the national speed limit was still 55 mph. A Trooper from the Nevada Highway Patrol was sent out to investigate the report of an early morning rollover accident on the I-15 just north of Jean, Nevada, located near the California/Nevada Stateline. Not given the exact location, the trooper investigated, quickly finding evidence of a possible accident in the form of a very long skid mark that peeled off to the right side of the road. Looking across the dark, barren region, the officer saw numerous pieces of a vehicle scattered about the desert landscape.

Off in the distance, he then saw a single car laying upside down, obviously the result of numerous rolls and turns. The trooper estimated the car must have been traveling well over a hundred miles an hour to have reached that distance from the road. Hastily moving towards the car, the trooper thought to himself that this could be a messy one as he counted at least six deep impressions in the soil where the vehicle had apparently impacted as it rolled and flipped. Arriving at the car, which was sitting on it's roof, the trooper pulled out his flashlight and shined it into the driver's side window. There, he discovered an Asian gentleman hanging up side down, suspended by his seatbelt. Seeing the man moving around inside, the trooper tapped on the closed window of the vehicle and waited for the man to roll it down. The trooper then asked the man if he was injured. Without hesitation the man replied, repeating the same words over and over—"I do 55, I do 55!"

Michael Nihei, Sergeant. Nevada Highway Patrol. Las Vegas, Nevada

ONE BANG UP JOB

Los Angeles County Sheriff's Deputy Ed Chenal may be retired now but, back in 1973, he was doing one bang up job. Working the day shift at the Norwalk, California Sheriff's Station, Deputy Chenal responded to a reported possible suicide attempt. The deputy was met at the door of a residence by the informant, a middle aged lady, who told him that the suicidal woman had apparently taken an overdose of prescription drugs and locked herself in the bathroom. Hearing this, Deputy Chenal quickly made his way to the locked door. After knocking on the door and demanding entrance several times with no response, he knew what had to be done next. Deputy Chenal turned to the woman who had called and told her that he would have to kick down the door to rescue the suicidal woman. Nodding her head in agreement, the informant replied, "Do what you must to stop her." Without hesitation, Deputy Chenal kicked the bathroom door with all his might, splintering it into pieces. When he looked inside, he found the woman sitting on the toilet. Seeing the deputy, the woman turned toward him saying, "Do you mind!" Quickly demanding that she come out of the bathroom when she had finished, the somewhat embarrassed deputy turned toward the woman who had made the rescue call and apologized for having to break down the door. To the deputy's surprise, the woman just smiled and said, "Oh, that's okay. I don't live here. I'm just a neighbor."

Ed Chenal, Lieutenant (Ret.). Los Angeles County Sheriff's Department. California

RUDE AWAKENING

In the late 1980's, long before St. Charles Parish, Louisiana, had the I-310 Bridge which connected the east bank of the great Mississippi river to west side, the only way to get across the river was by way of a ferryboat. The St. Charles Parish Sheriff's Office and Jail were located on the west bank, which meant that any arrest made on the east bank of the river would result in an officer escorted trip across the river on the ferryboat. One night while on his way back from dropping off an arrestee, a deputy sheriff drove his police cruiser onto the ferryboat. Pulling his car all the way forward as instructed by one of the ferryboat workers, he situated his cruiser right underneath a bright spotlight. Since the wait to cross the river was sometime as long as forty-five minutes, the deputy not bothered by the luminous from above, quickly dosed off, taking a well deserved nap in his unit. Meanwhile, on the east bank of the parish, a sheriff department practical joker thought it would be funny to key his radio microphone just as a passing train blew its whistle. Abruptly awakened, half dazed to the combination of the train whistle blaring across his sheriff's radio and the bright spotlight shining in his face, the drowsy deputy jumped from his squad car in a panic thinking he was about to catch a train the hard way. Talk about a rude awakening!

Barry Matherne, Deputy Sheriff. St. Charles Parish Sheriff's Office, Louisiana

JUST THE FACTS

Louisiana is the only state in the Union that does not have counties. Its political subdivisions are called parishes.

TAKE IT EASY

Buy them books, send them to school, and they still don't learn. That is something Robert Mueck is witness to everyday. As a Lieutenant for the University of Maryland Police Department, he can recall one particular night filled with such examples. The night started out with the usual large parties, followed up with the ensuing drunken fights, rounding out the evening with two officers from the plain-clothes detail making an arrest for an armed robbery. Wanting the detail officers to wind down from the stressful arrest, the men were told to walk around the high-rise dorms to "take it easy." As they entered the elevator, an over-eager college student, unaware of the officer's true identity, engaged them in conversation. For some unknown reason, the young man began telling the officers that he was heading outside to sell some drugs. The officers, in utter-disbelief, asked the student if they could tag along and watch. "Sure!" the unsuspecting student replied. A few minutes later, a drug transaction took place and the plain-clothes officers made the arrests. To say the least, the drug-dealing student was stunned at the officer's true identity. After all they had been through that night, the officers finally "took it easy" at the central booking office, laughing aloud at how easy the bust had been!

Robert Mueck, Lieutenant. University of Maryland Police Department. Maryland

THE POWER OF WORDS

In 1994, the World Cup of Soccer was being held in Pasadena, California, at the internationally famous Rose Bowl. The Los Angeles County Sheriff's Department had a large security contingent present for the event. Deputy Sheriff Dan Jordan was assigned to a riot suppression team and was staged in an outlining area, just a few miles from the Rose Bowl. Being that the Rose Bowl had limited parking; people were encouraged to park in lots away from the event and then take shuttle buses to and from the venue. At one such shuttle bus pick-up and drop off area, people were starting to get unruly and were pushing and shoving to get one of the limited seats on the bus. A bus driver, fearing for his safety, and for the safety of others, panicked and pulled away without any passengers. Deputy Jordan watched as the bus almost knocked a small group of event goers to the ground. Making their presence known, the riot suppression team Jordan was assigned to quickly brought the rambunctious crowd under control, restoring calm and order to the area. However, all their efforts were almost in vain when a senior deputy announced to the crowd via a loud speaker, "line up and be patient as there will be more shuttle buses by soon to run you over!"

Dan Jordan, Deputy Sheriff. Los Angeles County Sheriff's Department, California

TUG OF WAR

When it comes to tracking down criminal suspects, having a K-9 team on scene can be a very effective tool for fighting crime. Having two on scene, though, almost makes it seem unfair for the criminals. "Too bad," says Deputy Herman Foster and his German Shepard partner, Apollo. Called to a large junkyard filled with smashed cars, where the City of Roseburg, Oregon's police, had cornered a burglary suspect, Deputy Foster met up with another canine unit (Belgian Malinwa) assigned to assist with the call. Wanting to give the suspect a chance to surrender before unleashing the hounds, Foster got on his PA system, warning the man that he had thirty seconds to sound out his position or they'd turn the dogs loose, making sure to include that they would bite. As usual, the suspect didn't take him up on the offer. With the canine teams positioned at opposite ends of the junk yard, Foster and the other officer gave the "find" command simultaneously. Watching the two dogs set off on their given assignment, Foster thought to himself that there was nothing prettier than watching two dogs work so well together; that is until the two trained animals find the suspect at the same time. As if they were breathing the same air, the two dogs caught the scent of the suspect at the same time. Less than five minute later, they had him. Hearing the commotion from a distance, one of the deputies called out to the suspect to stop moving and the dogs would stop biting him. The suspect obviously didn't believe him because, when the two deputies arrived at the dog's location, they found them playing tug-of-war with the man, one having him by the leg, while the other was chewing on his arm. Seeing that the situation was well under control, the deputies took a minute to appreciate their canine's technique for subduing a suspect. Assured that the suspect was now in full compliance of their orders, they called off their dogs. With all said and done, the dogs ended up scaring the suspect so much that he completely relived himself of all his bodily functions. Luckily, for the K-9 units, that they don't transport prisoners.

Herman Foster, Senior Deputy (Ret.). Douglas County Sheriffs, Oregon

211

FAKING IT

Some people believe they can fake their way through life, and everything will be just fine. Unfortunately, all they really end up doing is making their life harder in the long run. Take in point the subject of our following story. A young man was arrested and taken into custody for an outstanding warrant out of Moorhead PD, Minnesota. During the booking process, the man mentioned that he had a history of seizures, and, at the time, was without his medication. Everything started out okay, the man proceeding through the booking process with little difficulties. As he went for his mug shot, however, the man suddenly collapsed to the ground and began seizing. This activity lasted approximately five minutes, and then stopped. After a short period of time, firefighters and an EMT unit arrived on scene to take over medical care. The man again displayed another bout of apparent epileptic behavior in front of them. This second act of seizing did not fool anyone, though, but with their hands legally tied, the EMT unit still transported. For legal and liability reasons, the man was released from custody prior to the transport, with the original warrant being reissued for his arrest. Once at the hospital, a doctor who worked on the patient called the jail and stated that the young man had admitted to him that he was indeed faking the seizures to get out of jail. At the time, this may have sounded like a good idea, faking the seizure to be released, but in reality, he just made things worst for himself. Not only did he still have the warrant out for his arrest, he now has a large ambulance and hospital bill to pay for. Nice move, Slick!

Adam Torgerson, Correctional Officer. Clay County Sheriff's Office. Minnesota

WHERE'S A COP WHEN YOU NEED ONE?

In 1975, Deputy Sheriff John Swensen of the Los Angeles County Sheriff's Department was working in an area well known for residential burglaries. There were so many burglaries in fact that he started preparing early in his shift by writing reports during briefing just to keep up. With another day beginning, Deputy Swensen finished his morning briefing and headed out to his assigned patrol area. Not soon after, he received a call to take another burglary report. With his clipboard in hand, Swensen knocked on the door of the reporting residence. A minute later, a woman answered the door, immediately pointing to a room and saying, "He's in there." Thinking, "Huh, this is just supposed to be a report call," Deputy Swensen asked the woman, "Who is where?" To which the woman replied, "My husband has him in the backroom." With his curiosity now peaked, Swensen cautiously walked to a backroom of the house. There he found an older man standing over a young juvenile male who was lying on the floor. With shaky hands, the older man was pointing a rifle at the youth, keeping him at bay. Peering up from the ground and seeing the deputy, the young juvenile graciously said, "I've never been so happy to see a cop."

John Swensen, Deputy (Ret.). Los Angeles County Sheriff's Department. California

CANINE CHAOS

A patrolman from a South Jersey Police Department had the common duty of making a notification to a resident. Arriving at the reported address, which just happen to be a senior center development, the patrolman knocked on the door and rang the bell several times, but he was unsuccessful in making contact with the occupant. What he was successful in, however, was in rousing a sleeping dog from within the unit that began barking angrily. With his concern for the occupant mounting, the officer decided to try to open the door and found it to be unlocked. Announcing his presence, he entered the apartment and was immediately attacked by a ten pound Schnauzer biting at his boots. While bravely fighting off the dog, he watched as an elderly woman casually walked by, oblivious to the situation. Finally, after winning the battle with the "attack Schnauzer" and getting the attention of the older woman (94-years), the patrolman tried to explain to her that he was looking for a man at this address. With the dog barking loudly, however, she was not able to understand him completely. The woman, becoming upset with the canine, began yelling, "Oh my God, why are you barking?" Trying to deescalate the situation, the patrolman attempted to secure the irritating dog. As he did, the frightened canine began defecating all over the floor. Getting increasingly frustrated by the situation, the older woman began pacing back and forth, stepping through the feces, and spreading it throughout the room. Eventually grabbing the dog, the patrolman secured it in a back room, but it quickly escaped. The woman then took her turn at trying to corral the animal, but the once loyal pet turned on it's owner, biting her upon her thumb. With blood spurring everywhere, the tidy apartment quickly took on the appearance of a murder scene. The chaos continued to build as the angry woman now began yelling at the patrolman, asking, "Why did you have to come here, the dog never does this?" Making her way to the bathroom to care for her injury, the old woman once again tracked through the fresh feces, spreading it down the hallway. Finally securing the dog for good, the patrolman went to assist the bleeding woman. He found her in the bathroom with blood smeared all over her face as she gnawed at a piece of torn flesh that hung from her thumb. Eventually getting a towel around the wound, the patrolman then suffered one last visual bombardment as the woman started picking up the dog poop with her blood soaked hand. To the patrolman's relief, a first aid squad quickly arrived, but not before the daughter of the woman returned home, only to stir things up all over again by yelling at her mom to get rid of the dog. In the end, the person the patrolman was looking for to begin with turned out to be in the hospital. All this confusion resulted from a simple and common task of trying to get someone to call somebody else who was trying to get a hold of them, who wasn't even there to begin with. If that isn't confusing enough!

Name withheld by request. New Jersey

JUST THE FACTS

New Jersey has the highest population density in the U.S. An average 1,030 people per sq. mi., which is 13 times the national average.

A BLOODY MESS

It seems that whether you are in a large metropolis city like Los Angeles, California, or even a small rural community such as Darby, Montana, first responders can not manage to escape the ugliness in the world. Arriving on the scene of one of the worst crimes to hit the small town of Florence in decades, a reserve officer for the Ravalli County Sheriff's Office prepared himself to see the worst, the results of a triple homicide. Instead of working the crime scene as he had anticipated, the deputy was instead directed to assist another officer at a disturbance call a mile away. Without going into detail, the disturbance call involved a very large, upset male and several pounds of very rotten ground beef. After a bit of a struggle, slipping around on said ground beef, the deputy arrested the individual and sent him to jail. Following the arrest, the deputy prepared to return to the homicide scene. Before returning, however, the deputy decided to try to get the very offensive ground beef out of the lugs of his boots. Stopping at an outside faucet in the middle of a shopping center, he began washing off the mess. As he finished, he looked up and saw several individuals poking their heads out of the surrounding businesses and watching him. By now everyone in town was talking about the triple homicide. Peering down at the mess of blood and meat on the ground, the deputy could only imagine what people were thinking.

A Reserve Deputy. Ravalli County Sheriff's Office. Darby, Montana

FINGER LICKING GOOD

As a first responder, we all know there may come a time in our career when we are called to go above and beyond the call of duty. Still, there are some lines that we hope we never have to cross. With this said, our thoughts of gratitude, along with a little sympathy, go out to Deputy Sean Gales of the Benton County Sheriff's Office of Sauk Rapids, Minnesota, for jumping on the proverbial grenade for the rest of us. Just arriving on shift, Deputy Gales was immediately called out on a medical call. Rolling up on scene, he found an elderly lady who had stopped breathing. Performing as he was trained, Gales pulled out an Ambu bag that he carried in his patrol car and began breathing for the patient. Unfortunately, he quickly found the bag to be inoperable. Figuring he had no other choice, Gales then began mouth to mouth resuscitation. Soon after, another deputy arrived on scene and began compressions on the still non-responsive woman. As he continued the rescue breathing, Gales bent down for another round of ventilations. Sealing his mouth around hers, he began to exhale. As he did, something flew out of the patient's mouth and into his. Immediately, Gales turned his head and spit the unknown object out of his mouth, much to the disgust of him and his now grossed out partner. Soon after, the ambulance crew arrived and took over the CPR. As he finished up the investigation of what had occurred prior to him being called, Gales interviewed the woman's male friend who was with her at the time she had collapsed. The man stated that the two had just returned from a well-known fast food chicken restaurant and that she had appeared just fine to him prior to collapsing. Once back at the station, the partner who was on scene with Gales approached him laughing, asking him how the chicken was today. Now every time Gales drives by the restaurant he can't help but think of that call, immediately losing the craving for "finger licking good" chicken!

Sean Gales, Deputy. Benton County Sheriff's Office. Sauk Rapids, Minnesota.

LIAR, LIAR, WALLETS A LITTLE LIGHTER

Some people will say or do about anything to get out of paying a traffic ticket, even lie. Detective Bob Mote of the Buena Park Police Department, has a warning for them, just don't do it in the Orange County, California Court System. In court to testify on a traffic violation, he was witness as a defendant explained to the judge that the reason he ran a red light was because he was blinking each and every time the red light flashed, making it impossible to see the red signal. Hearing this, the judge simply responded, "Thank you, sir. That will be one-hundred dollars, plus penalty assessment." The judge was not through, however. He then asked the man, "Do you really think anyone believes that's what happened?" Unaware of the consequences, the man replied, "Nope, but I had to give it a shot." Hearing this, the judge then said, "I'm sorry, sir. The fine is now five-hundred dollars, plus penalty. The extra fine is because you lied. I can't fine you any higher than the five-hundred dollars, but I warn you never to show your face in my courtroom again!"

Bob Mote, Lieutenant. Detective Bureau Commander, Buena Park Police, California.

JUST THE FACTS

The day of the week with the fewest felonious police fatalities is Sunday.

POLICE WORK IS NOT ALWAYS A BED OF ROSES!

Inquire of any police officer and they will tell you that law enforcement is not always a bed of roses. Just ask Officer Patti March of the St. Louis County Police Department. While enroute to a disturbance call at a well-known, foul smelling residence, she recounts a story told to her by a previous partner. The tale goes that after arresting and booking a man into the jail holdover, Officer March's former partner left the room to finish his paper work. Returning to the holding area a short time later, his nostrils were immediately assaulted by the fragrant smell of incense burning in the air. He turned and surveyed the room to find the prisoners in the cell "cowboyed up" with their t-shirts pulled over their mouths and noses in an attempt to cover up a foul odor. Inquiring of the source of the foul smell, the officer was answered by an angered station clerk, informing him, "the smell would be his prisoner!" Turning his attention towards the offending suspect, the officer noticed that the man he had earlier arrested had taken his shoes and socks off and was now walking barefoot across the cell, a strong stench emanating from his blackened feet. To make matters worse, the prisoner's toenails looked like bear claws protruding from the ends of his toes, clicking on the ground as he walked, proving that police work can sometimes really stink!

Patti March, Officer. St. Louis County Police Department, Missouri

TAKE ME TO JAIL, PLEASE!

It was just another beautiful summer night in Perry County, Tennessee. Highway Patrol Trooper Allan Brenneis was working the evening shift, on what so far had been an uneventful night. Patrolling Highway 13, one of his favorite roadways, Brenneis rounded a curve, meeting up with a pick-up truck traveling the opposite direction that had crossed the centerline by more than two feet. Swerving to the right to avoid the truck, Brenneis flipped on his flashing lights and turned his cruiser around in pursuit of the vehicle. To the officer's surprise, the pick-up immediately pulled to the side of the road. Exiting his vehicle and putting on his hat, Brenneis next observed the erratic driver getting out of his truck, and staggering towards him. Quickly sidestepping in-between the two vehicles to avoid colliding with the obvious intoxicated man, Brenneis watched with curiosity as the man stumbled past him, heading straight towards the back door of the patrol car. Knowing the man would be unable to open the locked door, Brenneis called out, "Sir, would you please step over here!" To which the man replied, "Why? You got me. Let's go to jail!" Taken back by his answer, the officer spent the next couple of moments trying to convince the man to comply with his request. Finally persuading the man to join him between the cars, Brenneis began his investigation, asking, "Sir, how much have you had to drink tonight?" The man quickly replied, "Too much, trooper. So let's go to jail." Doing his best to comply with the law, the officer then requested, "Well, sir. I'd like you to try a couple quick tasks for me." Shaking his head, the man answered, "Nope, don't need no tasks. You got me. Let's just go to jail." Loading the man in the car, Brenneis advised the man of his rights and asked him if he would take a blood test. Again, the man answered, "Nope, told ya, don't need no test. I know I'm drunk. Let's go to jail." Figuring further questioning would be pointless, Brenneis fulfilled the man's request and took him to jail. Flash ahead in time to the suspected drunk man's court date. Sitting in the back of the courtroom, Brenneis went over his testimony in his head. With no sobriety tasks performed, or blood test taken, flashes of doubt started to flood the patrolman's senses as to whether or not he had enough evidence to convict the man. To make matters worse, the man now sat quietly in the courtroom, smiling at him from across the room. This only put further doubt inside Brenneis, now thinking the man had been down this road before, and knew exactly what to do to walk free. Hearing the judge call the man's name, Brenneis sat up in his seat, paying close attention as the judge started the legal proceedings. "Sir, you are charged with driving under the influence. How do you plead?" asked the judge of the suspect. Looking up at the judge with a face as red as an apple, and wearing a smile like the cat who ate the canary, the man sluggishly replied in the same slurred tone as in the night he was arrested, "Your Honor, I was drunk then, and I'm drunk now, so let's go to jail!" ...CASE CLOSED!

Allan Brenneis, Trooper First Class, Tennessee Highway Patrol

JUST THE FACTS

There were more National Guard soldiers deployed from the State of Tennessee for the Gulf War effort than any other state.

THE PRICE OF FREEDOM

At one time or another, we have all paid an arm and a leg for an ATM surcharge. Deborah Mitchell, a Police Officer for the University of Maine, however, draws the line at fingers. One particular day, while assisting with a money escort at a nearby Credit Union, Officer Mitchell stood guard as a teller replenished the money inside an ATM machine. All of a sudden, some paper became jammed in the slot where the receipts came out. The teller, noticing the problem, started pulling on the stuck paper. As she was doing this, the machine unexpectedly seized her hand, pulling her fingers into the slot. Screams of terror started emanating from the teller's mouth, causing Officer Mitchell to quickly turn the power off to the machine. Without hesitation, the officer then began trying to free the woman's hand. Unfortunately, the machine had other ideas, keeping a firm grip on it's deposit. Knowing extra help was needed, Officer Mitchell contacted her dispatch center via her radio. She could only imagine what the person on the other end was thinking when she relayed the situation. After the request call, another officer responded. Instead of helping, though, he just stood there, staring in disbelief. Seeing this, Mitchell began yelling at him that she needed a pair of pliers, screwdriver, anything! A short time passed, and a large crowd began to gather, witnessing the woman's pain. Suddenly, a woman from the crowd stepped forward producing a pair of pliers from her purse. "Who'd of thought," contemplated Mitchell. Wasting no time, Mitchell began her assault on the machine. With bolts and springs flying, Mitchell was finally able to get to the part of the machine that held the stuck hand. Grunting like a wild boar, she pried with all her might, eventually winning the battle and freeing the woman. "Yeah," the crowd screamed. Soon after, an ambulance arrived on scene and transported the woman with minor injuries to the hospital. Mitchell's next dilemma, however, soon seeped into her mind—that of trying to explain to her chief why she just destroyed a $100,000 ATM machine. She first tried to call him on the phone, but he was not in. Late for a crew meeting, Mitchell decided to return to the office and try him later. As she walked into the conference room, she quickly noticed her fellow officers laughing hysterically and pointing to the chalkboard. Written upon it, in the chief's own handwriting, was the following: One money escort… free of charge. One trip to the hospital by ambulance…$45.00. Breaking a $100,000.00 ATM machine to free a teller…priceless!

Deborah Mitchell, Police Officer. University of Maine Police Department. Orono, Maine.

JUST THE FACTS

The coastline of Maine boasts so many deep harbors; it is thought all the Navies in the world could anchor in them.

Maine is the only state in the United States whose name has one syllable.

90% of the country's toothpick supply is produced in Maine.

TOUGH LOVE

Most experts would agree that in order to raise your child properly, you must sometimes resort to a form of discipline referred to as "Tough Love." Deputy Michael Shafer of the Lawrence County Sheriff's Office, may or may not agree with that statement, however, he does have one funny example of it to share with us. On patrol one night in Deadwood, South Dakota, Deputy Shafer had made arrangements to have his wife ride along with him. After several hours of patrolling the area, the two decided it was time for a coffee break. Pulling into a strip mall to visit an eating establishment that he visited frequently, Deputy Shafer was immediately flagged down by a man franticly waving his arms at him. Figuring he needed some help, Shafer pulled up to him and began gathering information. The man, who was a manager of one of the retail stores in the mall, told him that a red car had spun a lot of donuts in the parking lot, nearly striking a light pole in the process. The car then proceeded to the fast food restaurant across the way and was still parked there. Hearing this, Deputy Shafer went to investigate, driving over to where the car was parked. There he found the owner of the vehicle talking on his cell phone. Formally discussing his driving habits with the vehicle's owner, Deputy Shafer got the young driver to admit to his erratic driving behavior. Citing the man for exhibition driving, Deputy Shafer then returned to the manager of the retail store to tell him the outcome of the situation. When Deputy Shafer advised him that he had issued the young man a ticket, the store manager asked, "His name wasn't Tom Smith was it?" When Shafer told him it was, he then asked the manager how he knew that. The manager quickly replied, "That's my son. I forgot he just got that car today."

Michael Shafer, Deputy. Lawrence County Sheriff's Office. Deadwood, South Dakota

WITH TIME COMES EXPERIENCE

With time comes experience. Seizing an opportunity to train a new partner on the art of interrogation, Detective Chris Christopher of the Los Angeles County Sheriff's Department, along with his junior partner, started interviewing three detained auto burglary suspects. With the individual suspects separated into three different rooms at the station, the detectives went to work, quickly getting two of the suspects to admit guilt. The third man, however, was a little older, and wise to the system, already having prior felony convictions. The man just repeated his innocence, saying that he didn't know why his friends would say he was involved. He stated at the time of the alleged crime, he was sleeping in the back seat of the car and was unaware of his buddy's activities. Having an idea about what to do next, Detective Christopher excused himself, telling his junior partner he had to leave for a moment. This action confused the other detective because it was unusual to leave in the middle of an interview. More confusion was about to follow. Christopher returned a few minutes later, this time with a young woman at his side. She took one look at the suspect then turned to the detectives and said, "That's him." Thanking her, Christopher then told the woman she could leave. Feeling that he had been positively identified, the once reluctant suspect now admitted to several vehicle burglaries. Afterwards, Christopher's partner admitted to him that, at the time, he didn't have a clue as to why he brought a station secretary, who was not an actual witness or victim, into the interrogation room. This tactic proved to the new detective that with time comes experience, and to the suspect, the experience of doing time!

Chris Christopher, Detective. Los Angeles County Sheriff's Department, California

A HOLLYWOOD HELPING HAND

Southern California is a well known tourist destination. Due to a lack of public transportation, taxi cabs throughout the area prosper. While most taxi drivers are hard working and honest business people, there are many illegal ones driving "Gypsy" cabs. What makes these "Gypsy" cabs illegal is a lack of proper documents and county permits. One night in 1992, Los Angles County Deputy Sheriff Mike Ascolese was assigned by his captain to target these renegade cabs outside the famous "Roxbury" nightclub. Starting his patrol of the local hotspot, he noticed that the illegal cab drivers parked in groups of three or four, making them easily detainable. Confiscating licenses and registrations, Ascolese had his hands full citing frustrated cab drivers and having their vehicles towed away. Noticing that the officer was becoming overwhelmed by the growing line of agitated drivers, along with the mounting paperwork, a private citizen stepped forward, offering his assistance. Acting as his eyes and ears, the man kept close vigilance on the cabbies for Ascolese. Though he could see him through his peripheral vision, the deputy never got a close look at his helpful companion. A good hour passed when the Good Samaritan told Ascolese that he had to leave. Turning to thank him, the officer was more than surprised to see who he was. It turned out that his back up partner that night was none other than Bernard Schwartz, better known as the legendary Hollywood star, Tony Curtis.

Mike Ascolese, Deputy Sheriff. Los Angeles County Sheriff's Department, California

D. C. Shake Down

Just when Michelle Dillard, an officer with the Metropolitan Police Department in Washington, D.C., thought she had seen it all, one more thing always seemed to drop out in front of her. As she was riding alone, patrolling her area, she received a call for a possible assault on a security guard at a laundry mat. Arriving at the specified location, Dillard quickly noticed a man standing out in front of the business on the sidewalk. Stepping out of her car she was met by the security guard who identified the man as the suspect. Placing the man into custody, Officer Dillard did a quick pat down of the suspect, checking for weapons. Not finding any, Dillard called a male officer to perform a more complete search, and to transport the suspect. When the male officer arrived, Dillard brought her fellow officer up to speed of the situation. The male officer then began the pat down, eventually making his way down to the suspect's legs. There, he came upon a long, hard object on the inside of one of the pant legs. Thinking it could be a weapon or some sort of contraband, the male officer began vigorously shaking the suspect's pants in attempt to loosen the object. Observing this action, Dillard watched in suspicious curiosity as the unknown object slowing crept down the suspect's leg. With one last, good shake, the object fell from the suspect's pants revealing not a weapon, but instead a long, large and hard piece of feces. Talk about your shake downs!

Michelle Dillard, Officer. Metropolitan Police Department. Washington, D.C.

FARGO 101

The North Dakota State University Police Department consists of eleven personnel, ten of which are licensed police officers. All licensed officers are armed and have full arrest powers. To keep sharp, officers regularly attend specialized schools throughout the year to update their training and knowledge. There are some lessons, however, which are not taught in a classroom, but are learned the hard way. Fortunately, Officer Marc Baetsch of the NDSU Police Department was a witness, and not a student, to the following lesson. Responding to a reported person down call in a parking lot late one night, Baetsch and a partner, along with a team of paramedics, arrived on scene to find a young man lying face down in a pool of his own urine, his clothes completely saturated from his personal liquid. After a quick check-up, the paramedics determined the man was okay, just drunk. Baetsch and his partner now stood there, wishing they had a rookie with them so he could do the pat down search of the inebriated, urine-soaked man. From out of nowhere, a group of fraternity boys suddenly appeared, stating they were friends of the man and would take care of him. Picking him up by his arms and shirt, they stood him up and began walking him home, comforting the man by saying comments like, "It's okay, buddy. We got you." Walking a few steps, one of the men asked his intoxicated friend, "Hey, dude. Did you walk through a sprinkler or something? You're all wet!" Hearing the comment, one of the paramedics called out, "That's urine. Your buddy peed himself." Looks of horror flushed across the faces of the fraternity boys. The friends immediately dropped the man to the ground and began cursing loudly, while others pulled out their cell phone cameras and began snapping pictures, with promises that this would be all over the internet the next day. With the lesson now over, Baetsch and his partner drove off thinking that with friends like that, who needs enemies? Class dismissed!

Marc Baetsch, Police Officer. N.D.S.U. Police Department. Fargo, North Dakota

228

HEAD CASE

There is an old saying that no good deed goes unpunished. Just ask Pat Weeks, a retired sergeant with the Los Angeles County Sheriff's Department. Back in 1979, he was the watch sergeant on duty one night at the East Los Angeles Sheriff's Station. Suddenly, two surly type homicide detectives came walking through the back door of the station asking in a sarcastic tone, "All right, where's the head?" Trying to be helpful, the sergeant pointed the way to the bathroom, telling them to go down the hallway and through the men's locker room. A few minute later, the homicide detectives returned, explaining that they were not looking for the bathroom, but instead the "decapitated head" that was found earlier in the day and placed in the evidence refrigerator. To this day, Sergeant Weeks is unsure if the detectives truly believe he was being sincere in his directions, or that he was just trying to mess with their "head."

Pat Weeks, Sergeant (Ret.) Los Angeles County Sheriff's Department. California

JUST THE FACTS

The average age of officers killed over the last century is 38. The average length of service at time of death is approximately eight years.

LONG DISTANCE WIFE PROBLEMS

Police department communication centers receive hundreds if not thousands of calls each year. Most are legitimate in nature, requiring quick thinking and immediate dispatch of emergency services. Some, however, are examples of why people shouldn't be allowed in public unsupervised. Back in the mid 1960's, one such instance of this moronic behavior happened to Sacramento Police Department Officer Kevin Mulderrig. While assigned to the communications center, he received the following phone call from an irate husband. The man was complaining about his wife, saying that she was nagging constantly at him and that he wanted the police to come and take care of her. Noting the bad reception on the phone line and believing it was probably a long distance call, Officer Mulderrig asked where he was calling from. With confidence in his voice, the male caller replied, "Los Angeles." Hearing this, Officer Mulderrig questioned back, "Sir, do you know this is the Sacramento Police Department? Why don't you phone the Los Angeles Police Department with your spousal complaint?" Without hesitation, the man replied, "I did that. They told me that there was nothing they could do about it, and if I didn't like it, I should phone Sacramento (State Capitol) and that's exactly what I am doing." (In the emergency service, we call this action—job security.)

Kevin Mulderrig, Lieutenant. (Ret.) Sacramento Police Department. Service - July 1, 1958 – December 28, 1989

RABBIT VS. PIG

Some stories you just can't make up. One foggy night in a Mayberry type town in the seaside community of Charlestown, Rhode Island, Lieutenant Jack Shippee of the Charlestown Police Department, received a call for a single vehicle accident with a report of a woman screaming on scene. With Police, Fire and Rescue responding, Shippee arrived on scene to find a Volkswagen Rabbit sitting in the middle of a two lane blacktop, with steam pouring out from the engine compartment, the result of having collided with a 500 pound pig. Yes, PIG! Not only was the car totaled, it was also covered in pig manure. Seeing no signs of human injury, such as blood in the car or a shattered windshield, Shippee went in search of the driver. Following the sounds of distress through the heavy fog that blanketed the area, Shippee found the male driver and his female passenger on the side of the road, the female crying hysterically. Questioning the driver as to why the female passenger was so upset, the man looked at the police officer, then at his totaled VW, and then at his female passenger and whispered, "She's a Vegetarian."

Lieutenant Jack Shippee, Executive Officer. Charlestown Police Department, Rhode Island

JUST THE FACTS

Judge Darius Baker imposed the first jail sentence for speeding in an automobile on August 28, 1904 in Newport, Rhode Island.

THE LOOKOUT

In Los Angeles County, California, there is no prerequisite of high intelligence to become a thief. The following story starts out with two would-be-thieves planning to commit a residential burglary at a condominium complex. Agreeing on a plan of action, the "brains" of the operation stationed his partner outside, giving the lookout specific directions to whistle if he saw any law enforcement personnel. With his partner in position, the other man then entered the building, unaware that they were under surveillance by nearby neighbors. It wasn't long until sheriff deputies arrived, finding the lone lookout still standing outside, staring blankly at them as they approached. With no warning from his partner, the other thief then exited the building carrying the stolen goods. The suspects were immediately arrested and subsequently interviewed by detectives. It turns out the lookout was legally blind and that the "brains" of the operation knew this prior to assigning him his given task.

Chris Christopher, Detective. Los Angeles County Sheriff's Department, California

JUST THE FACTS

Most Sheriff's badges have six or seven points. On a seven point badge, it is believed the points represent the seven letters of the title "Sheriff," standing for Service, Honor, Ethic, Respect, Integrity, Fairness and Faithfulness.

THE "FINE ART" OF POLICE WORK

Police officers in general believe that humor is an essential tool in the fine art of police work. Officer Tom Rowe of the New York Police Department, would have to agree after having the pleasure of one day working with a partner who's comic relief helped pass an afternoon away. While on assignment in uniform in an unmarked police car, Officer Rowe and his partner stopped at an intersection. There, they noticed some local teens hanging out on the street corner. The juveniles, also noticing the police presence, acknowledged the officers with a quick nod of their head. Wanting to have some fun, Rowe's comical partner quickly grabbed his clipboard off the dashboard, and wrote the word "WANTED" in large black letters at the top of the attached blank paper. He then proceeded to draw a stick figure of a man below. Finishing the drawing, he waved the teens over. As they approached, he held up the picture, asking them in jest, "Have you seen this guy?" To his astonishment, the dim-witted teens questioned back, "Why, what he do?" Playing it for all it was worth, Rowe's partner responded, "He killed someone." Seeing that the teenagers still believed the joke to be real, the officer added one last comment. "If you see him, be sure to call the police." Surprisingly, they agreed. Officer Rowe and his partner then left the intersection, drawing from the comic relief the rest of the afternoon!

Tom Rowe (NYPD Retired)

JUST THE FACTS

New York Police Department has laid to rest more officers (580) than any other agency.

THE VALUE OF A GOOD EDUCATION

It was 6 a.m. on a cold, chilly Monday morning in 1981, only three weeks left until Recruit Officer Gary Chiurazzi was to graduate from the Los Angeles Police Academy. . ."Chiurazzi, I want to see you in my office, NOW!" Words that any police trainee would fear. Arriving at the instructor's office after an earlier verbal assault about his appearance at that morning's uniform inspection, Chiurazzi, noticed his instructor "Sarge" sitting at his desk with another officer standing silently in the corner. Sarge wasted no time beginning round two of the verbal assault. "Chiurazzi, what's your problem?" asked the instructor in a derogatory tone. "None, sir," the trainee replied. Sarge then asked, "Chiurazzi, what did you do before you "tried" to be a police officer?" "Sir, I attended college," was the recruit's answer. Sarge grumbled, "Well, you obviously didn't graduate." Chiurazzi replied, "Yes, sir. I did. I have a B.A. in Criminal Justice.

Sarcastically Sarge questioned back, "You're 26 years old, what have you been doing all this time?" "Sir, I attended law school," the trainee answered. "Oh, so you flunked out of law school. Is that it, Chiurazzi?" With cautious optimism, the recruit answered back, "No, sir. I graduated in three years." Unwavering, Sarge continued on, "You failed the bar exam, didn't you?" Chiurazzi went on to explain that he had taken the exam just prior to entering the academy, and that two weeks ago, he had received a notice that he had passed. At this point, the other officer in the room peered up from the newspaper he had been reading and began to laugh uncontrollably, saying, "Sarge, you better leave Chiurazzi alone. He's going to be your boss one day." Hearing this, Sarge sat back in his chair and with about as much kindness as a lion would portray to his prey, instructed Chiurazzi to rejoin his class. On the way back to his classmates, it dawned on the trainee that his mom was right about one thing—a good education is priceless!

Gary Chiurazzi, (Former) Police Officer. Los Angeles Police Department, California

UNIVERSAL TRANSLATOR

In such a diverse city as Los Angeles, California, it is almost essential to speak a foreign language, especially Spanish. Some employers even give bonus pay for such interruption skills. There is one language, however, that needs no translation, and Los Angeles County Deputy Sheriff Mike Ascolese is fluent in it. Responding to a backup request from a fellow deputy, Ascolese arrived on scene to find the requesting deputy sheriff holding four male Hispanics in a vehicle at gunpoint. The men weren't responding to the handling deputy's multiple requests, given in English, to exit the vehicle. Unable to speak Spanish, Ascolese instead headed for his patrol car to activate the "universal translator." Getting into the front seat of his unit, Ascolese keyed the microphone of his PA system, holding it between his knees to keep the mic on. He then removed his shotgun from its rack, placed it in front of the keyed PA mic, and quickly racked a round into the firing chamber. Through the miracle of translation, the four Hispanic males immediately exited the vehicle and placed their hands behind their head. Ascolese then turned to the handling deputy and explained to him that there are some languages that are universal.

Mike Ascolese, Deputy Sheriff. Los Angeles County Sheriff's Department, California

A STICKY SITUATION

Years ago, Deputy John T. Banks of the Los Angeles County Sheriff's Department, stopped a car for speeding. The young female driver was very polite, saying that the reason why she was speeding was that the night before, she had accidentally spilled a coke on the floor of her car. The next day she found the gas pedal of the vehicle very sticky, causing her foot to fuse to the accelerator, resulting in her speeding. Fast forward a year later, Deputy Banks was again on patrol in the same area, when he pulled over another driver for speeding. To his surprise, he found the occupant of the vehicle to be the father of the same young female he had ticketed a year earlier for the exact offense. Not wanting to show favoritism, the father also received a ticket. The court date was set. The father showed up, and gave the following explanation for the violation, "I spilled coke on the floorboard," he explained, "and my foot got stuck on the accelerator." This story proves that the apple doesn't fall far from the tree. Both were found guilty!

John T. Banks. Deputy Sheriff. Los Angeles County Sheriff's Department, California

JUST THE FACTS

When Stephen C. Foster was Mayor of Los Angeles in 1854, he resigned to lead a mob, which removed a notorious suspect from jail and proceeded to hang him. Foster was promptly reelected. Such was the tenor of the times.

DOG GONE IT

It is said that a dog is man's best friend; however, if you ask Private First Class Nick Cain, a Military Police Officer stationed at Fort Huachuca, Arizona, he might just disagree. While on patrol one day at the post, he received a call to locate a stray dog that was roaming the streets. Finding the dog quickly, PFC Cain approached the canine carefully. The large German Shepherd immediately started growling and barking at him, his sharpened teeth baring a warning to stay away. Not taking any chances, Cain swiftly drew his PR24 retractable nightstick from its sleeve. As he did, he accidentally struck himself on the knee with it, causing severe pain. Cain then watched as the frightened dog made his escape down the main drag of the post. Not wanting to lose the animal, Cain hobbled to his car and chased after it. With lights shining and sirens blaring, PFC Cain radioed for reinforcement. With multiple units now in pursuit, spectators watched as what appeared to be a dramatic car chase, simply turned out to be a stray dog out running the police, showing the rest of the world who the true master really was.

Nick Cain, PFC. 18th Military Police Detachment. Fort Huachuca, Arizona

JUST THE FACTS

The battleship USS Arizona was named in honor of the state. It was commissioned in 1913 and launched in 1915 from the Brooklyn Navy Yard.

237

HONESTY IS THE BEST COMEDY

While writing parking tickets outside a children's museum, Susan Hanson, a Parking Control Officer for the Bellingham Police Department, was approached by the owner of a vehicle she had just cited. With ticket in hand, the irate man started in on Hanson, demanding to know why she had written him a citation. Hanson replied that the meter he was parked in front of had expired. The man then explained that just because he was late coming back, he didn't necessarily deserve a ticket. The whole time this exchange was occurring, the man's four year-old son was standing at his side, trying to get his father's attention. Ignoring his son, the man continued his argument, adding that every time he parks downtown, he always puts money in the meter, and has never received a ticket. With the man done pleading his case, he then turned to his young son who was still trying to get his attention. Asking the boy what he needed, the boy replied, "But, Dad, you never put any money in the meter." Caught in his deception, the man suddenly went silent. Without saying another word, he picked up his son, jumped into his car, and left the area. Hanson, doing her best to remain professional, tried not to laugh, however, some moments are just too good to keep to yourself. A parking meter fee 50¢, a parking ticket $25, a young child's honesty—Priceless!

Susan Hanson, Parking Control Officer. Bellingham Police Department, Washington

MISTAKEN IDENTITY

Just remember if you mess up, stay positive, as things can always be worse. This is something Reserve Deputy Steve Pair never forgot during the remainder of his career after calling for back up on one particular call. On patrol in West Hollywood, California, with his partner in search of a triple shooting suspect, the two deputies were driving very slowly in their squad car. They had their lights blacked out and the doors to their patrol car open. Deputy Pair was driving with his weapon on the seat beside him. His partner, Deputy Leo Monahan, had his shotgun at the ready. With both deputies operating their spotlights, Deputy Pair suddenly inhaled deeply, while stepping on the accelerator of the car at the same time. Surging forward, Pair then quickly applied the brakes, bringing the moving vehicle to a screeching stop. Trying to catch his breath, Deputy Pair managed to stutter, "There is a man standing on the top of the garage and he was pointing a gun at me!" Hearing this, Deputy Monahan immediately called for back up, receiving everyone in the area except the Auto Club for a response. With all deputies now in position, someone shined a light up towards the area where the man with the gun was last seen. Instead of illuminating a shooter, though, the light was shined on a Los Angeles Dodger. What was thought to be a man holding a gun turned out to be a full-size cutout display of a Los Angeles Dodger with both his hands extended in front of him as if he was catching a ball. Later, Deputy Pair told another deputy how embarrassed he was about mistaking the replica ballplayer for a suspect. The other deputy quickly replied, "That isn't embarrassing. Embarrassing would be if you actually shot the damn thing!"

Steve Pair, Reserve Deputy. Los Angeles County Sheriff's Department. California
Leo Monahan, Reserve Deputy. Los Angeles County Sheriff's Department. California

RAIDER'S FAN

Before becoming the Director of Boulder Rural Fire-Rescue, Colorado, Kurt Gattmann was a police officer with the Coolidge Police Department in the state of Arizona. Located close by was an Indian Reservation. Whenever an Indian juvenile was arrested within the city limits, they would have to be returned back to the Tribal Police Station for detention. Late one night, while on duty, Gattmann arrested two male Indian juveniles for vehicle theft. Both individuals were very intoxicated and didn't speak English. The arrest soon became physical and violent. One youth quickly submitted after being handcuffed. Gattmann then had to contend with the other boy, who would not go as easy. Fighting with the juvenile, Gattmann was able to handcuff him and forcefully carry him over to the patrol car. Opening the back door, he then placed the youth in feet first, having to push the rest of his torso into the caged back seat. With the young man not wanting to give up the fight, Gattmann then had to use his full body weight, pushing his shoulder up against the back door to shut it. In route to the reservation, the one youth continued to struggle. He kicked and thrashed, screaming louder than a Raider football fan. Arriving at the Tribal Police Station, Gattmann asked one of the tribal officers why the youth was still so upset. Translating the juvenile's outburst, the tribal officer told him, "You slammed the door closed on both of his hands!"

Kurt Gattmann, Director. Boulder Rural Fire-Rescue, Colorado

STUPID QUESTION DAY

Working desk duty, Deputy John T. Banks of the Los Angeles County Sheriff's Department, was constantly bombarded by questions that really didn't pertain to law enforcement. Saturdays always seemed to be the worst day for these types of questions, thus deeming it: **Official Stupid Question Day!**

On one such day, a woman called and asked, "What are the weather conditions at the Magic Mountain amusement park?" Without hesitation, Deputy Banks swiftly replied, "The temperature is 78 degrees, humidity 63%. Winds are out of the south/southwest at 12 mph. Surf is fair, with 3-4 foot waves at eight second intervals, and there is a 60% chance of rain in the five day forecast." Irritated at his reply, the woman quickly snapped back, "Well, that's kind of a smartass answer!" and immediately hung up on him. Proving the old saying, "Be careful what you ask for, you may get it!

John T. Banks, Deputy Sheriff. Los Angeles County Sheriff's Department, California

JUST THE FACTS

In the City of Los Angeles, they have enhanced 911 services which offer many features unavailable in other areas. Enhanced 911 services automatically provide the emergency dispatchers with the telephone number of the caller, the address, the closest cross streets and map coordinates. Incoming calls are routed directly to the Police Department's dispatch center located underground at City Hall East. Calls for fire and medical emergencies are quickly transferred next door to the fire department dispatch center. The closest emergency resources are selected with the assistance of a computer and then dispatched.

BEGINNER'S LUCK

Remember the old adage, "If it can go wrong, it will." This particular saying was probably running through rookie Officer Sheila Lambie's mind the day she was asked to patrol the streets of St. Paul, Minnesota, in an unmarked police car. Fresh off of four months of field training and still in her probationary period, she was given the keys to the vehicle with the strict reminder to be careful because the car was assigned to a sergeant who was off duty that night. Beginning her routine patrol, she quickly stopped to assist another officer who was working a traffic stop. Seeing that the officer had the situation under control, Lambie continued on her way. All of a sudden, another car pulled out from a side street. With no where to go, Lambie's borrowed ride slammed into the passenger's side of the vehicle. Thoughts of panic raced through her mind, "crashing a sergeant's car, what else could go wrong?" Her answer soon poured out of the other car in the shape of a very intoxicated man stumbling towards her saying, "Officer, thank God you're here. That other car just hit me!" More misfortune headed Lambie's way as she discovered the drunken man's license had been revoked, and that the vehicle he was driving had license plates that didn't match the V.I.N number of the car. This would mean hours of reports for her. The only good part of this whole situation Lambie thought was that the man would soon be off the streets and heading for jail. With that day behind her, Lambie returned to work the next day to discover a number of job applications for different fast food restaurants in her mail box. To add insult to injuries, she also found out that the sergeant whose car she crashed had put out a "Stop and ID for criminal damage to property report, and her description was on it. What a way to start a career!

Sheila Lambie, Officer. St. Paul Police Department. Minnesota.

RUNNING ON EMPTY

In law enforcement, one makes contact in a variety of ways with all sorts of people. One day, while in a marked black and white police car, assigned to a non-related patrol / traffic enforcement duty, Dan Jordan, a Deputy Sheriff with the Los Angeles County Sheriff's Department, was passed by a car driving at least 15 mph over the posted speed limit. In the world of law enforcement, this is called a blatant disregard of police presence, or, "contempt of cop." Pulling the violator over, he approached the car, discovering an elderly female driver. He politely asked her if there was a problem or an emergency. She quickly responded, "Yes, I have a problem and an emergency...I am very low on gas and I'm trying to reach the next gas station before I run out."

Dan Jordan, Deputy Sheriff. Los Angeles County Sheriff's Department, California

JUST THE FACTS

In 1875, the first horse patrol trotted down the unpaved streets of Los Angeles. Personnel were paid $95 a month for their services, $5 more than the foot patrolmen and only $10 less than the City Marshal. The Department continued to deploy mounted officers until 1916.

WHAT ARE FRIENDS FOR

While on patrol in the County of St. Louis, Missouri, Police Officer Michael Moore Sr. was assigned to a disturbance call at one of the local "Popeye's Chicken" restaurants. Entering the building, Moore contacted the manager of the establishment and asked him what the nature of the problem was. The manager stated that he wanted a man, let's call him "Robert" for now, who was working inside, removed from the business. Finding the request not out of the ordinary, Moore approached Robert, who was fully dressed in a Popeye's uniform and told him his boss wanted him to leave. Moore then told the employee to step outside and wait for further instructions. Officer Moore returned to the manager and asked him what the problem was with the worker. The manager surprisingly answered, "I came in about three hours ago and saw this guy (Robert) setting up the cooking area. I had never seen him before, but I figured that another manager must have hired a new guy. As Robert was working, the other employees began conversing with him, and, to be honest, this guy works better than anyone I've ever worked with. He's fast, efficient, and I didn't have to ask twice for specific orders. I just felt like God had blessed me with another potential manager." Not seeing the problem, Moore again asked the manager why he wanted the man removed, to which the man replied, "Robert doesn't work here." A puzzled look washed across Moore's face. Asking the manager to clarify his statement, the manager continued, "Robert is the best friend of Derrick, who is an actual employee. Derrick couldn't make it in, and didn't want to get fired, so he asked Robert to fill in for him." The puzzled expression worn upon Moore's face turned to one of astonishment. "You got to be kidding me!" blurted out Moore. The manager quickly replied, "Nope." Unable to control himself, Moore burst out laughing. Eventually regaining his composure, Moore again stepped outside to find Robert in the same place he had left him. Robert then explained to Moore that he had received an earlier call from

Derrick, asking him if he could "fill in for a few hours" while he took care of something. Trying to help out a friend, Robert had run over to Derrick's house, got into his work uniform, and then showed up at Popeye's. (Talk about dedication to your friends!) Shortly after, Robert's friend, Derrick, arrived and was then fired and, guess what...Robert was hired and is now the newest manager. The funny thing about the whole situation is that Robert now won't rehire Derrick because of his unpredictability! What are friends for!

Michael K. Moore Sr., Police Officer. St. Louis County Police Department. St. Louis, Missouri.

JUST THE FACTS

The most destructive tornado on record occurred in Annapolis, Missouri. In three hours, it tore through the town on March 18, 1925, leaving a 980-foot wide trail of demolished buildings, uprooted trees, and over-turned cars. It left 823 people dead and almost 3,000 injured.

DR. RIGHT, I PRESUME

Sometimes even when you're right, you're wrong. Working an early morning shift, Deputy Chris Christopher of the Los Angeles County Sheriff's Department, received a 902A call, also known as a possible suicide attempt. Arriving at the reported address, Christopher and his partner made contact with the subject, a Mr. Wright. They quickly determined the man was severely depressed and that he wanted to talk to his Psychologist. Christopher promptly contacted the female therapist and asked her to respond to their location. With fire department paramedics now on scene, the two deputies walked outside and waited in their patrol car, finishing writing up some earlier reports. A short time later, a very attractive woman arrived, parking her car across from the officers. Thinking she was the psychologist, Christopher's partner leaned out the car's window and asked her, "Are you looking for Mr. Wright?" To the officer's surprise the woman returned the question with a strange look, replying, "No!" The woman then walked straight to the adjacent apartment and entered. Not long after, the actual psychologist showed up. This time, Christopher asked her the question, making it a point to carefully rephrase it to, "Are you looking for your patient?"

Chris Christopher, Detective. Los Angeles County Sheriff's Department, California

FAST FOOD FOLLIES

The following story is proof that "fast food" doesn't equal "quick thinking." Jim Smith, the Police Chief in Cottonwood, Alabama, explained that while working for another agency earlier in his career, he had the opportunity of dealing with the most stupid thief in history. The suspect, who was in his late teens, worked for a local fast food restaurant. One night, he decided to rob a convenience store near his home. Making a hooded mask by cutting eyeholes from a carryout bag from his workplace, complete with company logo, he walked into a convenience store, still wearing his work uniform, his nametag proudly displayed on his chest as he announced a robbery. The clerk, who immediately recognized the disguised suspect even with the bag over his head, tried to talk him out of the crime, but the dimwitted thief was not deterred. This prompted the convenience store worker to produce a pistol to further convince the misguided teen of his poor judgment. With the tables now turned, the frighten thief quickly fled empty handed. When the police arrived on the scene, the clerk informed them who the suspect was. With the police waiting patiently at the suspect's residence, he soon arrived home, still in uniform minus the bag, but out of breath and out of luck. Needless to say, it was an easy arrest and conviction putting an end to one stupid thief's fast food follies.

Jim Smith, Police Chief. Cottonwood, Alabama

JUST THE FACTS

Audemus jura nostra defendere is Alabama's official state motto. Translated it means, *"We dare defend our rights."*

HUMOR SAFARI

As a Deputy Sheriff for the County of Los Angeles, Glen Swanson occasionally embarks on a "Humor Safari" as he witnesses the funny, yet bizarre behavior of the people of Los Angeles. One such episode occurred as he was supervising a group of detainees at the Pitches Honor Ranch Detention Center. This one particular inmate loved to entertain his fellow roommates. "Crazy Freddie" as he was referred to, would sit on the toilet and brush his shaved head with the toilet brush from the adjoining toilet as he serenaded his other male dorm-mates with love songs. (Let's just say "Freddie" had trouble maintaining a relationship.) Another trip of the bizarre occurred as Deputy Swanson was patrolling the streets around Lennox Sheriff's Sub-Station, in Inglewood, California. Driving by a gas station, he saw a man standing by his Toyota pick-up pumping gas. The man was wearing a striped shirt and a pair of blue jeans. Now, none of this in itself was bizarre. What was different, however, was how the man was wearing the blue jeans down around his ankles. The man just stood there, bare naked from the waist down, pumping the gas. This behavior would go uninvestigated, though, due to Deputy Swanson responding to a priority call at the time. With some oddities, it is best not to ask why.

Glen Swanson, Deputy Sheriff. Los Angeles County Sheriff's Department, California.

NO ANIMALS ALLOWED

A college university campus can be an interesting place to work for a police officer. There, they have to enforce state laws and campus rules and regulations. Now it's true, college students are known for bending the rules, and harassment of those doing the enforcement is not uncommon. One night while patrolling the college grounds at the University of Vermont, Officer Patrick Flynn heard a male student yell out the window "PIG." Knowing animals were strictly against the rules, Flynn promptly investigated the situation, quickly locating the room of the possible offense. Knocking on the door, he was then greeted by two male students. He asked them if they were boarding an animal against university regulations. The bewildered students answered, "No." Officer Flynn then asked if he could check their room because he had just heard them yelling for a barnyard animal. The now frightened students complied with his request and the search was on. To the police officer's surprise, there were no pigs found. The male occupants were asked for identification, and then advised by Officer Flynn that he would be documenting the fact that they were calling to a pig in their room, but that they couldn't explain why they were doing such with no animal in sight. Without speaking another word, Officer Flynn left the now perplexed students feeling the university judicial system would have a good time reading this report!

Patrick Flynn, Officer. Department of Police Services, University of Vermont

ROLL CALL

Studies show that employers value a person with a sense of humor. One first responder, Officer Michael Moore Sr. of the St. Louis County Police Department is a beneficiary of this fact. In 2004, Officer Moore was the only African-American officer assigned to his precinct. Getting a late start to work one day, he knew that his lieutenant would be furious at him. Arriving at the station tardy, he walked into the room where roll call was taking place to find his lieutenant, along with the rest of his Caucasian colleagues, staring at him. The lieutenant glanced down at his watch, then back at Officer Moore Sr. asking him the reason for his tardiness. "Well, LT," Moore Sr. replied, "I was actually on time, but I saw a magazine when I was grabbing my soda at the gas station. On the cover it read, "All Black People Carry Knives." I then had to run to the sporting goods store to get one because I'll be damned if I'm gonna be left out." Hearing his reply, the entire room burst into laughter, and his lieutenant told him to sit down and join them. One of the benefits of good humor in the work place is that it creates and reinforces a sense of solidarity, be us white, black, or even late for roll call!

Michael K. Moore Sr., Police Officer. St. Louis County Police Department. St. Louis, Missouri

A ONE DOG SHOW

During his fourteen year career as dog handler, Senior Deputy Herman Foster has been through a lot, or at least in one case—half way through. One Friday night, close to midnight, Foster and his K-9 partner received a dispatch for a domestic violence call in progress. Arriving on scene at a low income apartment project, Foster found the apartment unit in question to be upstairs. Parking his car at the bottom of the stairs, he left his German Shepard, Apollo, in the car. Alone, Foster cautiously made his way up to the apartment, knocked on the wooden door and announced his presence. When he did this, he could hear a female occupant inside of the apartment cry for help. Acting quickly, Foster kicked the door to the apartment open. Unfortunately, as he did, his foot went right through the hollow constructed door, getting his leg stuck half way. With the door now open, Deputy Foster observed a male suspect severely beating a female inside the apartment. With all the effort he could muster, Foster attempted to free his trapped leg from the door, to no avail.

Doing the next best thing, Foster called to his dog Apollo for help. Luckily, Foster had left the window to the squad car open. In a flash, the large dog was upstairs taking care of business. The male suspect did his best to defend himself against the canine, but he was no match for the superior dog. Still stuck in the door, Foster called out to the man, telling him to stop fighting and the dog would stop biting him. The foolish man, however, only replied in foolish words saying, "I'm going to kill the dog." Not likely thought Foster as he watched his partner go to town on the man. Finally, Foster could hear sirens and backup arriving. As the other deputies enter the apartment, Foster called the dog off and the suspect was taken into custody. After the incident, Apollo the dog was very proud of himself, not of Foster, who had to be literally cut from the door to be freed.

Herman Foster, Senior Deputy (Ret.). Douglas County Oregon
S.O. Roseburg, Oregon.

DANGEROUS DAVE'S
LONG ARM OF THE LAW

Even though fiction is fun, sometimes the truth can be just as entertaining. Keep in mind as you read the following story that it is true! David Reddish is a veteran deputy with the Los Angeles County Sheriff's Department, working at the Lancaster Station. The station's patrol area is made up of hundreds of miles of open desert and small communities scattered throughout. After driving thirty-minutes from the station to get to his patrol area, Reddish was immediately dispatched to a call. The complainant was a man with a small ranch who was having problems with a dirt bike rider purposely riding by the edge of his property and spooking his horses, causing some of the horses to sustain injuries. As the man was explaining his plight, he and Reddish both heard a motorcycle approaching along the fence line. Reddish promptly jumped into his marked black and white sedan and went after the rider. As he followed the rider down a rough dirt road, he wished for his regular patrol vehicle, a 4x4 that was in the shop for service. With the rider pulling away, Reddish activated his red lights and siren. Instead of acknowledging the police presence and stopping, the rider sped up, making a run for it across the open desert. Soon the dirt trail got too sandy and rough for the sedan, forcing Reddish to break off the chase. Making his way back to the informant's ranch, Reddish kept a close eye on the rebel rider climbing a small mountain butte. Back at the ranch, two men came walking over from the other side of the property to meet up with the deputy and find out what was happening. The men were known to the informant as they rented a small hanger on his property for housing their Ultra Light aircraft. (Ultra Lights are small aircrafts looking much like a hang glider, but with a seat and small engine.) This fact intrigued Reddish who just happened to be a licensed pilot. Knowing he had to adapt and overcome, Reddish hatched a plan to commandeer one of the Ultra Lights and head toward the mountain in search of the law breaking rider. One of the pilots gladly handed over the keys to his aircraft and the other pilot asked if he could fly in formation with Reddish to be of assistance. Reddish readily agreed and the two set off, taxing down the small dirt runway cut into the desert. One by one they became airborne and quickly located the rider still sitting on the hill. Even though the rider noticed the planes overhead, he didn't pay much attention, instead focusing on the deputy's radio car parked at the ranch below. Communicating by a walkie-talkie system rigged up between the two aircraft, reddish explained the next portion of his plan to the other pilot. The pilot was to fly his aircraft near the rider and get his attention while Reddish circled around the mountain and landed his agile aircraft on a small dirt path nearby. Executing the move, Reddish landed safely and quickly started hiking up the path towards the biker. As he did, he heard the bike start up and by the sound, determined it was heading his way. Reddish hid behind a bush and waited. When the rider was about twelve feet away, Reddish jumped out from behind the bush and pointed his firearm at the rider, yelling for him to stop. The rider, caught off guard, panicked and stopped so fast that he crashed in front of the deputy. Reddish quickly searched the man for weapons and obtained his drivers license. Reddish then instructed the biker to ride down to his patrol car and wait, warning him that if he didn't comply, a warrant would be issued for his arrest. Reddish then flew the Ultra Light back to the ranch, wondering how he would ever explain this to his supervisors back at the station. The rider was issued a Misdemeanor Citation for Destruction of Flora and Fauna and sent on his way with the stern warning not to return to the area. Reddish was happy with the outcome and figured the man would simply pay the ticket and be done with it. He soon discovered how wrong he was when the man decided to fight it in court. On the day of the trial the courtroom was packed with defendants and subpoenaed law enforcement personnel. As luck would have it, the rider's case was the first on the docket. At the beginning of the case, Reddish could sense that the Judge, being so used to the same old traffic testimony, wasn't keying in on the unusual facts. About half way through the testimony, though, the Judge looked up and said he had missed a part and to start again. The Judge then sat on the edge of his seat and listened intensely. During his testimony Reddish could hear little comments and laughter coming from his fellow law enforcement friends and the other defendants in the courtroom. The rider's only defense was, "The cops are always harassing us." The Judge found him guilty and fined him over one-thousand dollars. After this story made its rounds, Deputy David Reddish was given the nickname of "Dangerous Dave."

David Reddish, Deputy Sheriff, Los Angeles County Sheriff's Department, California

SAFETY BULLETIN

CHILD SAFETY ON THE INTERNET:

As a parent, if you own a home computer and allow your children Internet access, you also need to be Internet literate. If you do not know how to access the Internet, take a class, read a book or spend time with your children and let them show you the amazing world of cyberspace. Be aware of what is out there and prevent your children from gaining access to inappropriate web sites and chat rooms.

SUCH A DEAL

If the shoes fit, you have to admit…it's a good deal! One morning, Detective Chris Christopher of the Los Angeles County Sheriff's Department, listened as one of his fellow detectives began bragging about paying only $20 for an expensive pair of Italian shoes at an outlet store. Knowing the rest of his team needed some serious help with their fashion statements, especially Christopher, who frequently wore cowboy boots, the thrifty detective offered to take the team another day to the place where he had bought the designer shoes. A few hours later, the bargain hunting detective was sitting in his office, his feet up on his desk, reading over some reports. Sitting across from him sat the team sergeant, observing him closely. Using his years of experience as an investigator, the sergeant quickly determined the reason for his subordinate's great shoe deal. With as much diplomacy as possible, the sergeant pointed out to the detective that his shoes were not as great of a deal as first thought. It turns out that each shoe had a different sole pattern, proving the old adage; *if a deal sounds too good to be true, it probably is.*

Chris Christopher, Detective. Los Angeles County Sheriff's Department, California

"If the police never find it, is it still a clue?"
-George Carlin

OF MICE AND MEN

One evening in the fall of 2000, Bart Perrier, a Sergeant with the Osage County Sheriff's Office, was on duty working the evening shift, accompanied by a reserve deputy. It was approximately 11:45 pm and approaching the end of their shift when a police officer from a small town within the county contacted their unit. The officer requested the deputies to back him up on a residential burglary call with the possibility that the thief was still there. When Sgt. Perrier arrived at the reported address, he quickly recognized the informant as a frequent visitor to the county jail. The informant said he arrived home to find the front door wide open and his guns were missing from the gun rack. More importantly, he said he heard someone moving around in the house. Carefully, the law enforcement personnel entered the old two bedroom house. As they did, the stench of the poorly kept residence immediately attacked their sense of smell. Every area of the house was covered with trash thrown about, making the dangerous search for the suspect revolting too. At a bedroom door, Sgt. Perrier temporally halted the search as they all stared into a room that resembled a makeshift garbage disposal. The room was literally filled with hundreds of trash bags full of garbage, and the sound of little mice rummaging around could be heard. The smelly room was not going to deter Perrier from completing a thorough search for the suspect. Taking one long cleansing breath, Perrier entered the room, suddenly realizing there was no floor as it had rotted out long ago. With his flashlight in one hand and his duty weapon in the other, he made his way to a back closet, pushing trash out of his way as he moved. As he inched through the debris towards the closet he noticed a pair of hands in the corner. In a commanding voice he ordered the suspect out into the open. The other two backing officers figured he was just joking with them as no one would want to be in the dark, mice infested, trash filled room for more than a minute. However, the suspect really did exit the closet surrendering, and was quickly taken into custody for burglary. The missing guns were also recovered in the closet. It turned out the suspect and the victim were once friends and that the suspect came to steal some property in lieu of money the victim owed. The neighboring officer thanked the deputies a hundred times for helping and said he would never have expected someone to have really been in the house, especially in that room!

Bart Perrier, Sergeant, Osage County Sheriff's Office, Oklahoma

JUST THE FACTS

On the evening of March 25, 1948, a tornado roared through Tinker Air Force Base (AFB), Oklahoma, causing considerable damage, a few injuries, but no fatalities. However, the destruction could have been much worse. A few hours earlier Air Force Captain Robert C. Miller and Major Ernest J. Fawbush correctly predicted that Atmospheric conditions were ripe for tornadoes in the vicinity of Tinker AFB. This first tornado forecast was instrumental in advancing the nation's commitment to protecting the American public and military resources from the dangers caused by natural hazards.

SELF ANNIHILATION

Investigating a possible burglary can be a dangerous assignment for a police officer. At anytime, someone or in some cases, something, can jump out and surprise you. One night in West Hollywood, California, while investigating a possible break-in at a clothing manufacturing facility, a Los Angeles County Deputy Sheriff made his way carefully through the unlocked building. Rounding a corner, the deputy was suddenly confronted by an image of a man pointing a gun at him. Fearing for his life, the deputy aimed his already drawn service revolver and fired. With a feeling of self annihilation immediately draping over him, the deputy watched as the image of the now familiar man shattered into a hundred small pieces. It turns out the image was not another man, but instead a reflection of the gun toting deputy himself in a full length mirror. Great shooting, Tex!

Steve Pair, Reserve Deputy. Los Angeles County Sheriff's Department. California
Leo Monahan, Reserve Deputy. Los Angeles County Sheriff's Department. California

THE HOLE TRUTH

While working for the Multnomah County Sheriff's Office in the 1970's, Deputy Dennis Griffiths remembers a story about a "hole" which was still making the rounds from the 1960's. A "hole" is a place where graveyard shift officers would park their patrol car out of site and catch a few winks in-between calls. In the 60's, the patrol units didn't have the light bars used by today's patrol cars, but instead, had a single dome light that was lovingly referred to as a "bubble gum machine." This ever lasting story happened around Halloween time to a patrol car equipped with such a light. The story goes that a couple of scheming deputies creped up on a patrol car with two fellow deputies sleeping in their hole. Carrying a large pumpkin with a hollowed out bottom, the jokesters quietly slipped the carved Jack-O-Lantern over the dome light and then left undetected. They then called the dispatch by phone, letting them in on the joke, and had them dispatch the pumpkin unit on a code three call to a busy part of town. Trick or treat!

Dennis Griffiths, Deputy. Multnomah County Sheriff's Office, Oregon

THE POWER OF OBSERVATION

Good police work requires strong powers of observation. While patrolling his area for the Multnomah County Sheriff's Office, Deputy Dennis Griffiths spotted a man who was wanted on a warrant. The suspect was walking with a lady friend when Deputy Griffiths recognized him and made contact. Griffiths told the man he was under arrest and ordered him to stand by the trunk of his squad car and spread'em. The suspect immediately complied with the deputy's order. Griffiths opened the back door of the patrol car and then frisked the suspect. After the pat down, Griffiths reached for his handcuffs. When he did, the suspect suddenly took off in a sprint. Knowing he would never be able to catch the rabbit, Griffiths yelled to the escapee to come back and not get any additional charges against him. He did this even though he knew the advice wouldn't do any good. Sure enough, the suspect kept on running. Keeping a good eye on the direction the man ran, Griffiths jumped into his car to put out an assistance call for additional patrol cars. Sitting down, he systematically grabbed the door handle to close the door. He then turned forward expecting to find his radio, but instead found the prisoner compartment screen inches from his nose. His keen powers of observation quickly alerted him he was not in the front seat, but in the back. Luckily, his quick reflexes were able to stop the back door from closing just an inch before it shut. He knew that if he had closed the door or if the suspect's female companion had gave it a nudge, he would have been locked in the prisoner compartment. (Keep in mind that this was a time (circa 1970's) when deputies didn't have a radio on their hip, no cell phone, and no communication other than the radio in the driver's area screened off from the back seat.)

Griffiths quickly jumped out of the back seat noticing the suspect's friend laughing like crazy. When Griffiths got into the front seat, the whole scenario came into perspective for him and he too burst out laughing hysterically, now unable to broadcast the event. Continuing to laugh, he figured that with his keen powers of observation, he'd just find the suspect another day.

Dennis Griffiths, Deputy. Multnomah County Sheriff's Office, Oregon

JUST THE FACTS

Oregon has more ghost towns than any other state.

CLICK

Dennis Griffiths recalls the good old days of the early 1970's with fond memories. That was the time he was a deputy with the Multnomah County Sheriff's Office in the State of Oregon. He remembers working a graveyard shift in a rural area when "nature called." He safely parked his patrol car and walked into the woods to relieve his bladder. Upon returning to his vehicle, he unfortunately found the car locked, with the keys securely inside the car. Being an experienced deputy, he didn't panic as he knew he had wisely left his repeater on and would be able to get a radio call out. The portable radios deputies wore could only broadcast to their repeater housed in the trunk. When a deputy made a call on their portable radio it would be obvious to the dispatcher and the other cars, as there would be an extra click on the air, signifying the use of the repeater. Coming up with a plan to rectify the situation he now found himself in, Griffiths called his dispatch via his hand held radio and requested an adjacent district car to meet him at his location. Being a common call in law enforcement, he hoped it would conceal the fact that he just wanted the arriving deputy to help open his locked car. However, an astute dispatcher hearing the familiar click of the repeater told the responding unit, *"County 8, you might want to take a coat hanger with you, it sounds like he is on repeater!"*

Dennis Griffiths, Deputy. Multnomah County Sheriff's Office, Oregon

THE "WE TIP" TIP

Since the inception of the "We Tip" program" in 1972, police departments across the country have received over 300,000 crime tips. These tips from concerned citizens have resulted in over 12,000 arrests, over 6,200 convictions and the seizure of more than 300 million dollars in illegal drugs. Sometimes, the program works so well, even criminals tip off themselves. Investigating a vehicle burglary ring in Santa Clarita, California, Detective Chris Christopher of the Los Angeles County Sheriff's Department, received information on a suspect in the area. Not having enough evidence to obtain a search warrant, Detective Christopher did a routine background check on the suspect. Finding that the individual was on probation and had a search and seizure clause (Surprise), Christopher followed up with a probationary search of the individual's home. He didn't find any vehicle burglary evidence inside; however, he did find a number of stolen city signs, including a "We Tip" sign. The suspect was promptly arrested and charged with receiving stolen property.

Chris Christopher, Detective. Los Angeles County Sheriff's Department, California

INFORMATION BULLETIN

The We Tip Hotlines are 1-800-78-CRIME, 1-800-47-ARSON and 1-800-87-FRAUD and are available 24 hours a day, 365 days a year to report crimes.

THE WAITING

*A woman understands home fires burning…
lamps in window's porch lights.

Her patience forgives dinners spoiled, sleep interrupted
parties she goes to alone.

There will be other parties…love is a once-a-lifetime thing.
Food grows stale but Love keeps.

She has faith in his idealism when even he doubts it ——
she champions his causes when he himself is silent.

A woman understands that fear is only the wail of a siren in the
night and calm is the sweep of his headlights across the yard, the
turn of his key in the lock, the touch of his hand on her pillow
once again.

by Linda Syverson-Dent

*(Linda Dent is the sister-in-law to Oregon State Police Senior
Trooper Robert Dent (**Ret.**) from Bend, Oregon. She wrote this poem to
honor Bob's wife, Kathy and other officer's wives. *For reprint permission write to Robert Dent at: **Dent@Survival-Spanish.com** *copyright
1994 Linda Syverson-Dent)

BRANCHING OUT

The Los Angeles County Sheriff's Department is the largest in the world. It has the responsibility of protecting a population of 10,226,506 as of January, 2005. This county's population is only exceeded by eight other states. The county is made up of a very diverse population making the job for the deputies more challenging, dangerous, and sometimes even funny. In the mid 1980's, Deputy Alice Scott was working an early morning (graveyard) shift on the desk at Carson Station. At the time, Cason shared its radio frequency with the Lomita Station, which could cause the radio traffic to be very busy, with lots of exciting and potentially dangerous calls. One day, close to Christmas, and shortly before midnight, the air waves were unusually quiet for both stations. Suddenly, a Carson unit announced on the radio that he had "emergency traffic." When this kind of call comes in, all other routine traffic transmitted by the other units will be put on hold, allowing all deputies in the area to listen to the priority call in case they need to assist. The deputy with the "emergency traffic" broadcast was given an open microphone, keenly aware that all his fellow deputies in the area were now listening. The statement he broadcast caught everyone off guard. He said, "I'm in pursuit of a Christmas tree!" Moments later, the out of breath deputy put out a second broadcast, again saying, "I'm in pursuit of a Christmas tree!" Los Angeles County Sheriff Deputies are a very proud group and pride themselves on being highly trained and in good shape, so there was no way a tree was going to outrun one of the county's finest. Sure enough, the $5 grocery store tree was caught, along with its unlawful benefactor. That day, the Christmas tree bandit learned more than a $5 lesson. On the other hand, it was nothing compared to the even higher price paid by the deputy for his unorthodox radio transmission.

Alice Scott, Captain. Los Angeles County Sheriff's Department, California.

LANGUAGE BARRIER

The number one key to a successful relationship is good communication. In the world of first responders, nowhere is communication more important than between a K-9 handler and his dog. With hundreds of hours going into the training of theses animals, these effective crime fighters follow their handler's commands without question; that is, if they can understand what they're saying. A K-9 handler and his dog, Fry, in Roseburg, Oregon, found this out the hard way. Newly assigned to each other, Fry, a hundred-pound German Shepherd, and his human partner were called out to track down an armed robbery suspect. Quickly hunting him down, Fry alerted his human partner that he had found the suspect near a river bank, smack down in the middle of a briar patch. Fry's partner called out to the man not to move and Fry would not attack. Stupidly, the suspect responded with some choice four letter words, choosing to run instead of surrendering. Fry's handler quickly gave him the order to attack and off the dog went. With ease, Fry went over the bank, unlike the handler who fell down it becoming tangled in the briar patch below. As he tried to untangle himself from the mess he now found himself in, the handler could hear the obvious sounds of Fry having caught the suspect. Eventually freeing himself, the handler, along with two other deputies, one being the shift commander, made their way to assist their K-9 partner. Arriving at the dog's location, the men observed Fry in complete control of the suspect. Lucky for the man, he had been wearing a heavy foul weather jacket with a hood which was zipped and buttoned protecting him from any serious dog bites. Fry had a good hold of that hood and was dragging the suspect all over the rocks on the river bank. The watch commander listened as the K-9 handler called to Fry, giving him the "out" command. Fry didn't comply. He continued to drag the man around. Now, you may think the reason why Fry didn't listen to his handler was because he was not trained properly, however, it was more where he had been trained than how. It turns out that Fry was trained in Germany, learning his commands in the German language instead of English. In all of the excitement, the handler had forgotten the German word for "out," allowing Fry to remain in the attack mode. Luckily for the suspect, another officer arrived, giving the handler a quick refresher course in German. Even though Fry had taken the man for a good ride, the suspect was unharmed.

Herman Foster, Senior Deputy (Ret.). Douglas County Sheriffs, Oregon.

JUST THE FACTS

Oregon and New Jersey are the only states without self-serve gas stations.

The Tillamook Naval Air Museum is housed in the world's largest wooden clear-span building.

Eugene was the first city to have one-way streets.

SGT. "RICO SUAVE"

Officer Diana Johnson of the California Highway Patrol may not be an expert in vintage cars; however, she certainly knows enough to tell the difference between a 1960's model Studebaker and a 1980's model Toyota Corolla hatchback. On patrol on the south bound I-5 freeway in Southern California, Johnson exited the freeway coming to a complete stop at the bottom of the off ramp. Stopped directly ahead of her was a red, 1980's model, Toyota Corolla hatchback. Immediately, the sixth sense that most cops have kicked in and something told her to further investigate the vehicle. Quickly running the license plate on her mobile digital computer (MDC), the return advised her that the license plate belonged to a 1960's model Studebaker. Seeing this information, she then advised dispatch of her situation and requested another unit respond to her location so that she could effect a traffic stop. With the light turning green, the vehicle made an immediate left turn into a parking lot and stopped, with the CHP unit behind it. After her back-up arrived, Johnson and one other officer began to approach what appeared to be a female driver and female right front passenger. Coming up to the driver's window, Johnson got a good look at the driver who was wearing black fishnet stockings, a very short red mini skirt, and a low cut, black, sleeveless shirt. She also noticed the driver had on numerous items of costume jewelry and beautifully painted fingernails. Notifying the driver of the reason for the traffic stop, Johnson was caught by surprise when she heard a very deep toned, male voice coming from the tiny "female" looking driver. Upon closer examination of the driver, Johnson realized that SHE had an Adam's apple and there was hair poking through the fishnet stockings. Johnson's partner leaned over the top of the vehicle and whispered, "Well, that's not a bad looking woman, but that sure is one ugly man!" (Further investigation proved that the right front passenger was actually a woman.) After composing themselves, the two officers detained both parties and placed them inside separate patrol vehicles.

After much confusion with dispatch, they were able to run the VIN number from the vehicle and ascertain that it had felony wants associated with numerous burglaries through the Los Angeles Police Department.

Now, for the really funny part. That day, the two CHP Officers had a particular sergeant working who was well known to be quite the ladies man. Everyone knew his reputation and that he was quite proud of it. During the course of this investigation, Johnson heard that he was responding to the scene. Johnson and her partner then decided this was a perfect opportunity to play the world's best practical joke on the sergeant. When he arrived on scene, the two officers approached him, and gave him the Reader's Digest version of the stop (excluding the true gender of the driver.) Her partner told the sergeant that the "woman," who was driving, said that she knew him and she wanted to speak with him. Hook, line and sinker, the sergeant walked over to the patrol vehicle that contained the driver. Of course he wanted to make sure he looked his best, so he ran his fingers through his hair, straightened his gun belt, and primped in preparation. The sergeant approached the patrol vehicle and opened the door, making the driver's outfit VERY visible. The sergeant then looked at the driver and said, "So, you know me? What can I do for you?" The driver answered back in his low, manly voice, "I don't know what you are talking about." At that time, Johnson and her partner were now a few feet away laughing hysterically and uncontrollably. Needless to say, the only thing they heard from the sergeant that night was something to the effect of, "I'm gonna kill you, two!"

Diana Johnson, Officer. California Highway Patrol. Los Angeles, California

SLIPPERY WHEN WET

Southern California is well known for its picturesque sun filled days. Every once in a while, however, a few storm clouds manage to work their way down from the north, bringing with them a little rain. On one such raining day, Deputy Vicky Jelalian of the Los Angeles County Sheriff's Department, just happened to be on duty. The uniform for the day luckily included extra large yellow slickers and large rubber boots to protect her from the elements. Unfortunately, this outfit also included the path to her eventual downfall. With over six inches of water covering Pacific Coast Highway, in Malibu, California, the deputy responded to a silent alarm at a large two story home owned by a famous Hollywood star. With her partner at her side, the two met up with their sergeant a couple of doors down from residence. It was quickly decided that Deputy Jelalian would make first contact since she was a trainee at the time. As the group of deputies cautiously approached the residence, they discovered the front door wide open. Deputy Jelalian's heart raced thinking about the possibility of capturing a burglary suspect in a house of a celebrity. "TRAINEE!" the patrol sergeant bellowed. "You go in first!" "Yes, sir," the rookie deputy responded. With it still raining cats and dogs, Deputy Jelalian drew her gun and proceeded under the canopy that covered the front door. With the sound of the pouring rain lessened from the cover of the canopy, the deputies became acutely aware of sounds coming from the inside of the house. "Someone is in there," Jelalian whispered to her training officer. "Go check it out. I'm right behind you," he replied. With every step she took the sounds inside the house grew louder. The noise seemed to be coming from the kitchen area. "Go get'um!" her training officer whispered. With her heart racing, Jelalian swiftly ran across the marble floor towards the kitchen door. "FREEZE! SHERIFF'S DEPARTMENT!" she yelled as she slipped on the wet marble floor, sliding helplessly into the kitchen. As she did, she looked back at a man standing by the kitchen counter, putting down a grocery bag. "FREEZE! SHERIFF'S DEPARTMENT!" she yelled again as she landed on her stomach, arms stretched out at her side, legs raised in the air, still sliding across the floor, looking more like a small aircraft than a deputy sheriff. With a loud thud she landed, butt end up, against the wall on the other side of the room. With her hood over her face and covering her eyes, she couldn't see which end was up. All she heard was her partner and sergeant laughing and the man saying, "Oh, Officers. I am so sorry. It must have taken me too much time to turn off the burglar alarm. I just wanted a glass of wine when I got home." Not long after Deputy Jelalian found her pride and straightened herself out, her sergeant introduced her to the handsome owner. She then got his autograph and left the premises as soon as she could.

Vicky Jelalian-McKown, Sergeant. Los Angeles County Sheriff Department. California

JUST THE FACTS

Established February 3, 1855, "The Los Angeles City Guards," who, during their short-lived career, were attired in the City's first official police uniform.

WHAT'S IN A NAME?

Well, just ask Officer Randy Klopfenstein of the California Highway Patrol. While on patrol in Burbank, California, he received a radio call from another unit requesting help. This particular unit had pulled over a car occupied by a pregnant woman, which, as luck would have it, was now in active labor. Being fresh out of EMT school, Officer Klopfenstein raced to the scene to help. There he discovered a young woman screaming words in Spanish. Not speaking the language, however, being a master of interpretation, Officer Klopfenstein soon discovered the fact that the woman was already a mother of two wonderful children, making the present situation even more pressing. With the ambulance on the way, he quickly began his examination of the patient. Suddenly, and without warning, the floodgates opened as the woman's water broke and just three minutes later, Officer Klopfenstein was holding a brand new baby boy in his hands. Now, most would think the story would end here; however, there was still one more chapter to this story to be written. After a short interview, a Spanish news crew who interviewed the two after the incident asked the mother what she was going to name the baby. The mother decided that her new baby boy would take home a small part of the officer that helped bring him into this world, his name. Randy Lee Delgado (the baby) and family will forever be indebted to Officer Klopfenstein. Even years later the two keep in touch, just recently meeting again at the boy's high school.

Randy Klopenstein, Officer. California Highway Patrol.

This is not

THE END

But, only the beginning

We are already gathering stories for our next book

"First Responders Handbook of Humor- Second Alarm"

So, if this book helped you recall a story in your career; please take the time to submit it to our websites. And, as before, if we publish your story, we will send you a free copy of the book when it's released.

www.QuietManPublishing.com

www.FirstRespondersBook.com

RESOURCES

World Wide Websites: (Does Spiderman have a web site?)

www.hometown.aol.com/fireriter - History of Black Firefighters by Chuck Milligan, Retired Fire Captain

www.hometown.aol.com/fireriter1 - Early Black Firefighters of North Carolina by Chuck Milligan, Retired Fire Captain

www.Dr911.com - The premier multidisciplinary healthcare service for emergency public safety personnel.

www.willrogers.org - Will Rogers American Satirist

www.odmp.org – The Officer Down Memorial Page, Inc., is a non-profit organization dedicated to honoring American's fallen law enforcement heroes.

www.curiousquotes.com - Quotes on all subjects

www.aath.org - American Association of Therapeutic Humor

www.paramedics-ems.com - This is a website geared for anybody interested in getting into ems, or is already there. It has some practice tests; some humor pages, as well as photos of car crash extrication series.

www.ptsdpeace.org – The mission of the PTSD Alliance is to support PTSD (post traumatic stress disorder) survivors by advocating for their rights in the American society; finding assistance for them through public and private resources; and to educate the public on the effects of PTSD on the survivor.

www.nleomf.com – The mission of the national Law Enforcement Officers Memorial Fund is to generate increased public support of the law enforcement profession by permanently recording and appropriately commemorating the service and sacrifice of law enforcement officers; and to provide information that will help promote law enforcement.

www.tearsofacop.com – Dedicated to promoting educational awareness on the epidemic of law enforcement PTSD and suicide.

www.NationalCops.org - Concerns of Police Survivors, Inc. (COPS) provides resources to assist in the rebuilding of the lives of surviving families of law enforcement officers killed in the line of duty as determined by Federal criteria. Furthermore, COPS provides training to law enforcement agencies on survivor victimization issues and educates the public of the need to support the law enforcement profession and its survivors. It also provides peer support for survivors, national counseling and training programs, psychological counseling for children of slain officers, assistance to agencies in the development of procedures for line-of-duty deaths, and educational grants for spouses and children.

www.NCJRS.org - National Criminal Justice Reference Service (NCJRS) is a reference service provided by the National Institute of Justice, the research arm of the U.S. Department of Justice. Information specialists conduct literature searches of subjects related to law enforcement, including law enforcement stress.

www.50states.com – Find interesting facts on all 50 states.

www.rd.com. Reader's Digest - Submit your original humorous story (100 words or less) to Reader's Digest by printing you name, address and phone number and mailing to Humor, Reader's Digest, PO Box 100, Pleasantville, New York 10572-0100. All contributions may be edited and cannot be acknowledged or returned.

www.QuietManPublishing.com - For all your publishing needs

www.InfoMagic.Biz - Magical Motivational Messages

BOOKS:

Kicking Your Stress Habits by Donald Tubesing, PhD

Anatomy of an Illness by Norman Cousins, 1979

Healing Power of Humor by Allen Klein, 1989

Being Happy by Andrew Matthew, 1990

Heart, Humor and Healing by Patty Wooten, 1994

Practice Safe Stress with the Stress Doc: The Art of Managing Stress, Burnout and Depression by Mark Gorkin, C.S.W.

ABOUT THE AUTHORS

DAN JORDAN

BALANCE UR LIFE –
YOU'LL ALWAYS WIN!

Soon after graduating from high school with honors, author, Dan Jordan joined the U.S. Army. After fulfilling his service commitment and receiving an honorable discharge, Dan entered the field of law enforcement where he now has over 20 years as a Deputy Sheriff for the Los Angeles County Sheriff's Department. Dan lives in Southern California with his wife, Lisa, and two children, Justin and Alison.

BUL–YAW!

In addition to his law enforcement career, Dan is also a Professional Magician and Motivational Speaker.

Some of Dan's Motivational Message Topics:

- The Magic to Balancing Stress

- Stepping Out of your Comfort Zone

- The A.I.R. of Personal Safety

- Public Speaking 101 / Effective Communication Skills

Clients who have experienced Dan's mesmerizing, humorous and motivational messages include; California Highway Patrol, Dole Fresh Vegetables, Inc., Arizona Court Reporters Association, Costco Wholesale, Los Angeles County Fire Department, Northeast Valley Health Corporation….among others.

For more information about Dan, his magic shows or speaking programs and availability, or to request a booking, please contact: Dan@InfoMagic.Biz   www.InfoMagic.Biz

JOHN B. HICKS

The author of three other books, John is currently working on finishing his fifth and beyond. With more than twenty years with the Los Angeles City Fire Department, John resides in a small suburb of Los Angeles with his wife and children, where he is hard at work gathering ideas for his next adventure in writing.

In the effort to expand the minds of young readers, John also lectures at schools of all grades, spreading the importance of reading and writing. If you are an educator or organization, and are interested in booking an appearance, please contact him through the following website **www.QuietManPublishing.com**

OTHER BOOKS AVAILABLE BY JOHN B. HICKS
for the Future First Responders in Your Family

**TO ORDER BY MAIL SEND THIS FORM
ALONG WITH A CHECK OR MONEY ORDER PAYABLE TO:
Quiet Man Publishing
27542 Berkshire Hills Place #102
Valencia CA 91354**

Please send me:

____copies of "The Ghost of Fire Company 18"   @$6.50 per copy

____copies of "My Buddypack   @ $5.99 per copy

____copies of "Divided World   @ $6.50 per copy

Name: _____

Address: _____

City_____ **State**_____**Zip**_____

Phone Number_____

Email: _____

**WE PAY THE TAX. FREE SHIPPING
Also available through your major booksellers
or for more information visit our website at
www.QuietManPublishing.com**

For Personal Notes

For Personal Notes

For Personal Notes

For Personal Notes

For Personal Notes

For Personal Notes

WHAT ARE YOU STILL READING FOR?
THAT'S ALL YOU GET FOR $14.00